Lyrical Poetry

Lyrical Poetry

By Gold Record Songwriter/Recording Artist

Dan Clark

CFI
Springville, Utah

© 2007 Daniel Mark Clark
Dan Clark and Gene Pistilil for "Walk in Their Shoes"
Dan Clark and Monty Powell for "The Man I Would Have Been" and "Did You Know"
Dan Clark and Peter McCann for "Don't Let This Chance Go By"
Dan Clark and James Marsden for "Give My Heart to You" and "You Need a Woman Not a Song"

ISBN 13: 978-1-59955-048-0

Published by CFI, an imprint of Cedar Fort, Inc., 2373 W. 700 S., Springville, UT, 84663
Distributed by Cedar Fort, Inc. www.cedarfort.com

Cover design by Nicole Williams
Cover design © 2007 by Lyle Mortimer
Typeset by Kimiko M. Hammari

Printed in the United States of America

10 9 8 7 6 5 4 3 2 1

Printed on acid-free paper

Contents

Acknowledgments

For my special teachers who believed in me when others wouldn't: Ms. Dubois, Mrs. Inman, Dr. Morray, Mrs. Smart, Principal Richards, Mr. Croft, Mr. Thorem, and Coaches Din Morris, Brooks, Allen, Wageman, Trost, Martin, Weight, Simons, Banker, Zimmer, McBride, and Gadd.

For Russ Anderson, Don Pugh, Doug Miller, Fran Peak, Dick Nourse, Zig Ziglar, Jim and Karen Koeninger, Norm Gibbons, Lila Bjorkland, Micky Fisher, Jennifer Lapine, Ernie Wilhoit, Don Wilson, Kay Baker, Pat Mutch, Steve Cosgrove, Les Hewitt, Don Gale, Michael Gale, Chuck Coonradt, Charles Reid, Steve Munn, Wayne and Ruby Clark, Paul Clark, Kelly Clark, Gen. Hal Hornburg (Ret.), Maj. Gen. Johnny Weida, and Laura Calchera (Supreme Commander) for helping me launch my career and/or take it to the next level.

For my National Speakers Association inspiration: Mark Victor Hansen, Jack Canfield, Gail Larsen, Naomi Rhode, Dave Gordon, Robert Henry, Renee Strom, Keith Harrell, Roger Crawford, Bubba Bechtol, Grady Jim Robinson, Jim Tunney, Jeanne Robertson, Bob Murphy, Patricia Fripp, Ray Pelletier, Max Dixon, Mark Sanborn, and Art Berg.

For Bill Kimball, Bob and Paul Mendenhall, Dick Clissold, Bill Gibbs, Jay Jensen, Bob Raybould, Lincoln Hanks, President Royden and Sister Derrick, Phillip Gibson, Mark Tuttle, Gary Mangum, Scott Buie, Mark Monsen, Mont Beardall, Blain Hope, Todd Petersen, Colin and Theresa Dunne, Brendan and Evelyn Gibley, Todd Morgan, Brad Morris, and Brent Bowen for your spirituality, commitment to obedience, faith, and influence in my Christian walk with God.

For K.C., Danny, Nikola, McCall, and Alexandrea for finding wisdom, comfort, laughter, and solace in my speeches, stories, anecdotes, and words. I love you and need you in my life forever.

A Real Man

(Sung by a woman)

I need a man
Who knows happily ever after
Is a day at a time proposition
A man who knows makin' love
Is not a three-minute composition
It's a slow dance, full of romance
A walk on the beach in the sand
It's having a whole conversation, just by holding my hand
He would stir deep desire, that sets me on fire
To be with him all that I can
No, no I won't settle for anything less than a real man

A real man's strong in stature
Firm in faith and kisses slow
He sometimes cries, and when we hug
He's the last one to let go
Worshipping the ground I walk on, he's my biggest fan
There's nothin' like being loved by a Real Man!

I need a man
Who knows honoring me and my dreams
Is a macho disposition
A man who knows "I love you"
Is a more than words rendition
It's roses for no reason, secret love notes in my drawer
It's making me his equal, yet he always gets my door
He would never raise his hand to me, believes in who I am
Yeah, I can be more than I thought I could be, with a Real Man

You talk to me through touch
I'm swept away in every clutch
We're lovers but we're best friends too
I like me best when I'm with you . . .

Absence Makes the Heart Grow Fond of Other Things

They say when life's confusing, oh just get away
Join the restless looking for themselves in Santa Fe
They say a change in jobs, in neighborhoods
Will make things right
A geographic relocation helps you see the light

They say when you're not here you learn
To appreciate their love
Thinkin' somehow separation makes her
Who you're thinkin' of

But absence makes the heart grow fond of other things
Out of sight, when the cat's away, means out of mind
And mice will play, with all that brings
Absence makes the heart grow fond of other things

She says she wants to be alone, to think it through
Comparing notes with other women
Hearing what they'd do
They say to leave him, kick him out
Don't trust, say you don't care
You're better off without him
There are bigger fish out there

They say you're strong when things go wrong
If you can walk away
Thinkin' time apart will be the start of
Gettin' him to stay

In the absence of emotion, you won't ever change
In the absence of commotion, you can't rearrange
So bring it on, it makes you strong
Stay amidst the stormy weather
You must weather it together
Even if the sticks and stones you've thrown
Still hurt and sting . . .

Ain't Seen Nothin' Yet

Twelve October Daddy passed away
I wish I could have been with him that day
I was in Seattle, he was sick in bed
He had battled six long years, health hangin' by a thread

Mama sat beside him, pain was clear
He touched her tenderly and shed a tear
He could not speak, he was too weak, but lifted up his head
And with his dying breath and smiling eyes he simply said

If tears could build a stairway, and good memories a lane
I'd walk you up to heaven so together we'd remain
But I must go, it's how life flows, yet leave with no regret
'Cause we laughed and loved and lived each day
Like you ain't seen nothin' yet

Snow to snow the seasons pass on by
I miss my daddy's wisdom, sometimes cry
I am left to prove myself, and he is up above
He passed the torch of service on, a legacy of love

Mama and our family's left to cope
But families are forever, God gives hope
Dad lived to do, was never through, from morn to late to bed
He gave more than he took right till his last breath
When he said . . .

You ain't seen nothin' yet is 'bout the home stretch, final lap
The final inning, fifteenth round when
You've got to close the gap
I miss my Dad cause he lived his life
Like it's match point every day
And the same was true when he died
He ain't seen nothin' yet, I saw him say

Always Remember, Never Forget

There are only twelve notes in music
Classical, country, or rock and roll time
The difference between each melody
Is the order of notes and the rhythm and rhyme

We are life's writers, composers each day
Arranging to leave no regret
There are twelve notes of happiness, peace, love, and joy
Eleven to always remember
One to never forget

Be strong
Hold on for one more day
Press on with courage
And hope will light your way
Wish upon a star, remembering who you are
Cause you're here for a reason, regardless the season
To go beyond what seems too far

Stand tall
For something more than you
Be kind and giving
What you give comes back to you
Trust and be trusted, and pray to your God above
Eleven things to always remember
And never forget to love

Yes, twelve single notes in music
"A" through "G" played as a chord or as one
A hit song is born out of passion
With the same notes in bad songs that never get sung

Twelve notes of happiness, peace, love, and joy
We arrange to leave no regret
Eleven to always remember
And one to never forget

Artists of Being Alive

They express the inexpressible, without paint, guitar, or clay
They see and never have to draw, they feel what others say
What their presence touches, increases life itself
Not having only being, on a journey not a shelf

They don't just fix what's broken, create what needs to be
Tied in with God's graced perfect plan, fulfill their destiny

They preach only what they practice
Through inner peace survive
They neither sculpt nor hammer
For deeper purpose strive
They smell the roses, feel the love
With childlike wonder thrive
They never have to prove their worth
They are the Artists of Being Alive

They can heal a heartache with a glance or gentle touch
Their smiling eyes cry empathy, the worth of souls is much
Whatever seems to happen, they focus on the now
Forgiving life and what goes wrong, real happiness they vow

They don't judge outward covers
Impressed not with what seems
They're open to the universe, ambassadors of dreams

Reverently, quietly, they're life's true perfect tens
They always leave their jobs and friends
In better shape than they found them

Back Off, Barbies

(Sung by a woman)

The night was growin' old and the pickins gettin' slim
The thought of goin' home alone was startin' to sink in
But suddenly, like in my dreams, the door swung open wide
And in he walked, a cowboy god, a stallion in full stride
He paused and smiled and stretched his legs
And flexed his guns and back
Then swaggered over to the bar and ordered up a Jack
Three city girls with pumps and curls
So out of place and groove
Started to surround him and sprang to make their move

You're groovy, boss, hip, fab, clean, out-of-sight
Bodacious, bad, fresh, fly, moves so tight
You're cool, cocky, gnarly, fine, strutting so free
Hot, da-bomb, handsome, starched, decked to the tee

Yeah, they gawked and yeah they drooled
But I stopped their fantasy
And yelled, "Back off, Barbies, guess again, this stud muffin
Lord of Love is ending up with me!"

He smiled and nodded, tipped his brim
And chug-a-lugged his drink
Then headed to the dance floor, all hearts began to sink
The first tune spawned a country swing
The next ol' Cotton Eyed Joe
Song by song he tore it up from boot scootin' fast to slow
He nearly died when the steel slide cried
The fiddle made him weak
It was plain to see, the country twang
Was the only sound he'd seek

Be Is the Beginning of Become

Do you think you need a change
Do you think you can escape when you just move or rearrange
No matter where you go, or who you're with
Still there you are
Changin' color of the outside paint doesn't change the car

And trying to be someone that you're not is wrong
You have your own music so don't sing another's song

You gotta be, before you have or do
Becoming is your purpose, knowing who and why you're you
Now is new and new is now, "to be" the time has come
Be is the beginning of begin,
Be is the beginning of become

Who are you, and who were you born to be
Successful or a bum, we're all the same at the age of three
Don't give up when you still have something to give
Do not die before you're dead
'Cause you sold your reason to live

Step by step you'll find yourself
Through toil and strife
By living life one day at a time
You'll live all the days of your life

You're a child of the universe
Supposed to be here, vow
You'll make a lousy somebody else
Begin, become, be now

Be Who You Is

A father came home straight from work
And laid more work sheets out
His little boy didn't understand what deadlines were about
Dad told him he would need an hour
Then they'd swing the bat
But his little guy didn't understand
"An hour, how long's that?"

So Dad took out a magazine and found a photograph
Then ripped it in a hundred pieces and ripped them all in half
Dad thought it'd take him half the night
To make the puzzle whole
But his little guy came right back in, accomplishing his goal.

"How'd you get it done so fast?" he'd foiled Daddy's plan
"On the flip side of the world," he said
"Was a picture of a man . . . when I got the man right
It was plain to see, when I get the man right
The world is right for me."

His daddy smiled and said, "You're right
To you you must be true
If you keep trying to be like me, then who's gonna be you
You'll make a lousy somebody else, so be who you is
'Cause if you is who you ain't, then you ain't who you is!"

Ten years later, Dad still workin', home with papers out
His teenage son had come to know what deadlines were about
Graduation, movin' on, his eyes were full of tears
He hadn't spent much time with Dad, his future full of fears

He asked, "Dear Dad, how much you make?
What for one full hour?"
Proudly he said, "Hundred bucks
I climbed the corporate tower."

His son walked out and got his savings bond
He'd saved for school
"I'd like to buy an hour of your time just by the pool."

Guilty tears began to flow, "I've blown it bad, my son
I've sold out chasing dollars, I tried to be like everyone
I should have been my own man, it's what I always teach
I should be more like you, son, and practice what I preach."

Father, son began to run and share themselves at last
They lived a lifetime every day and made up for the past
And the secret to their closeness was just being who they is
'Cause if you is who you ain't, then you ain't who you is.
If you is who you ain't, then you ain't who you is.

In Two More Days, Tomorrow's Yesterday

I used to live my life on time delay
A day behind, a day ahead, but never right away
Hurry up and wait was a road rage waste of time
Fast, slow, stop, going out of my mind

Tomorrow is the day I thought would never come
Yesterday and "used to be's" are when I got me some
The older I get the better I was, memories change
The only constant's what we rearrange

Past, present, future—really are the same
Different order, separate times, all the same game
What will be makes history, this too shall pass away
In two more days, tomorrow's yesterday
Past, present, future—all turn to day
In two more days, tomorrow's yesterday

Today is the someday I longed for yesterday
Wait until tomorrow was the cheapest price to pay
The other side seemed greener, talked of glory days of play
Was caught between tomorrow and yesterday

They say timing's everything—what should be will be
Things happen for a reason, it's a lifetime guarantee
What goes around comes back around
Just by a different name
The more things change, the more they stay the same

Big City Blues

Two falls ago I struggled, just to keep the farm afloat
'Cause the price of wheat had plummeted, a banker's sour note
I did my best to keep the herd, but the price of beef went bust
The farmer's life is work and pay, no profit isn't just

So I finally caved into my debt, I had no other choice
Became a city slicker with a cowboy's heart and voice

Yeah, I'm a cowboy, singing the blues
Yeah, I'm a cowboy, singing the blues
I'm country from my roots, from my hat down to my boots
I'm a cowboy with the big city blues

My friends they came to visit, just to see the way I feel
Cement and smog are all around, this jungle's too unreal
They can't believe what's happened
To the family, church and school
What happened to strong values, and the mighty golden rule

So to remind me of the good old days
They filled my yard with hay
And brought turkeys, charlet bulls, and pigs
To shoot and ride and play

Time has tested all of us, all governments now know
The life-blood of a nation begins with what they grow
They spent a bundle on the bomb
While people starved and stare
But through it all we've heard the call
That food shows how we care

So never ever lose the truth 'bout agriculture's worth
'Cause cowboys are the most important workers on this earth

Yeah, I'm a cowboy, whoopin' the blues
Yeah, I'm a cowboy, whoopin' the blues

I've bought another farm, have regained my country charm
I'm a cowboy who's whooped the
Bank's three-piece suit wearin', middleman's seldom sharin',
   Politicians shallow swearin', foreign policy never carin',
   Investors' shaky darin', low prices forever blarin',
High interest always starin', world hunger constantly glarin', While
   my fences need repairin'
Yeah, I'm proud to be a cowboy
A cowboy whoopin' the big city blues!

Busy Doing Nothing, Naturally

Drivers start your engines, yes I heard the corporate call
The rat race started, winning was the goal for one and all
Faster, faster pushing from the lead I could not fall
And gradually I lost control and crashed into the wall

Everything I'd worked for burned in flames, went up in smoke
But the only thing I asked for was my family when I woke
The wreckage of my life was towed away with all my stuff
And my something now was nothing
But my nothing was enough

They say if you can't do something nice
Don't do anything at all
So I'm busy doing nothing, since my something hit the wall
I totaled out my fast lane life, got a new priority
What once was nothing now is something very dear to me
So I'm busy doing nothing, naturally

I'm now relaxed, a motivated mass of indirection
My only thrill is when I chill, no longer need perfection
The speedy me, you'll never see
Just watch the wheels go round
Contented fellow, loose and mellow, finally I've unwound

My racing days were just a phase of insecurity
Competition proved my worth, the checkered flag was money
Then something changed, had nothing left
To lean on, hold and love
But with nothing left to lean on
There's just one thing I think of

Daddy's Little Girl

(Sung by a woman)

Today I stumbled and spilled on the floor
And I haven't cleaned my room in a week or more
Most parents go ballistic, will my father be mad
Daddy forgive me, I've been bad

There's no such thing as a bad girl
Things you do may push my world
But a father's love remains unfurled
No matter your way, at goodnight we will play
Eskimo Butterfly Curl
Even when you're old and gray, I'll always say
You're Daddy's little girl

Today the teacher yelled, "Grow up," and made us feel blue
Please, sir, that's what we're all tryin' to do
When I make mistakes I always feel sad
I sure hope no one thinks I'm bad

As life moves me onward I've learned not to fear
'Cause I figure God's like my dad down here
The way we relate to our Father above
Is taught through our dad's unconditional love

Dance with Me

Friday night at Billy Bob's a lonely man walked in
I leaned against the pillar as the crowd began to thin
As the dancers two stepped 'round I felt so out of place
Then suddenly across the room I saw an angel's face

Nervously, I thought about the things I'd like to say
And when she looked around at me she took my breath away
We'd been together for so long but ended in a fight
I hadn't seen her in so long, her smile lit up the night

Our fingers touched and then held hands
We'd try again to trust
This long time love affair was so much more than shallow lust
The music mellowed magically
The dance floor lights went low
And as she cuddled close to me I whispered so she'd know

Hold me tight
Don't fight the feeling flow
Squeeze with might
I've missed you, oh I need you so
We had set each other free
But the stars align, we're meant to be
Life's a dance, oh baby, dance with me

The melody had ended long ago but we hung on
We didn't want this dance to end, the night became our song
The party all but disappeared, the place was closing down
And we were left alone to feel the new love we'd just found

The silence filled our hearts with hope that we could carry on
Then the singer softly offered may we play again your song
I knew this dance was one more chance to open up and show
So I kissed her gently on the neck
And whispered so she'd know

Did You Know?

(Man/Woman Duet)

Man
Did you know that I am lonely
Can't you see my heart is broken
Can't you tell I need a shoulder to cry on
Is there anybody out there who cares, who knows?

Woman
Did you know that I am waiting
Can't you see my heart is open
Can't you tell I'll always hold you and love you
Yes there is somebody out there who cares, who knows

Love sees the light in the eyes of a stranger
Love climbs the walls, never thinks of the danger
Love heeds the call of a thousand angels
Lives of quiet desperation
When all hope and inspiration's gone—love lives on . . .

Man
Did you know that I am hurting
Can't you hear my pain's unspoken
Can't you feel that I've stopped dreamin', believin'
Is there anybody out there who cares, who knows

Woman
You feel like you're alone in a crowded room
Well so does everybody else
If you've got the strength and if you'll take the dare
Just look into the eyes of the people sitting there
And love them—just love them
Let them love you

Dogs Never Lie about Love

I think I'm going out of my mind
Still searching for the perfect love, the one most never find
Venus women, men from Mars, our differences defined
Yet here we are, still playing games
The same lame rules, the same old grind

Where is real, I yearn to feel, connection blessed above
We should show, what canines know
Dogs never lie about love

Dogs never lie about love
Open, unconditional, honest, never fictional
When I'm home, she wants me like a cold hand needs a glove
Will not judge, won't hold a grudge
When tough times come, she stays, won't budge
When I'm gone, I'm the one she's thinking of
Dogs never lie about love

She's always there to greet me at the door
I'm her most important guy, the one that she adores
The later I am the more excited she gets just for me
And doesn't care about past loves, examining with jealousy

She accepts me just the way I am like God above
Canines know true loyalty, dogs never lie about love

Dogs forgive, forget the past
Know what it takes to make love last
If they could talk they'd tell us life without true love's a crime
Dogs are always happy cause they're loving all the time

Don't Let This Chance Go By

Have you ever had the feelin'
That time was in your hands
Then you put time off until another day
Life can't live without you
Take your dream and make it real
Before the magic of this moment slips away

Don't let this chance go by
Dig down deep inside you
Find the faith you can't deny
You'll never know if you don't try
Don't let this chance go by

If you look beyond the questions
No mountain can't be moved
And you'll live your life in a place you've never been
Every new day is a doorway
So open just as wide
'Cause you know you'll never pass this way again

Some never take their chance of a lifetime
In this lifetime of chance
They live their lives with music inside them
But never really dance
They hope to be happy but since they hope
They never really are
Being and becoming stay afar

Dreamin' at the Blue Bird Café

It all begins with a song
Tonight I feel your love so strong
Your eyes say, "yes, you can, my man"
Your smile says, "you're my biggest fan"
My voice cracks, yet you clap, still sing away
Cause it's songwriters night at the Blue Bird Café

Dreams are for sale at the Blue Bird Café
Somewhere an artist is one hit away
So I take the twelve notes found in music I play
And with my guitar rearrange them each day
Yes many a melody spread forth its wings
And flew up the charts to stay
It all begins with a song
Dreamin' at the Blue Bird Café

It all begins with a song, I sing
Painting pictures lyrically, ballads are my thing
Your open heart says soothe my soul
Your reaching out makes love our goal
Together we'll leave knowing life's okay
'Cause it's songwriters night at the Blue Bird Café

DeeDee tells the world we're wonderful most every night
So we strive to fill the billing
We connect through music's might
I sing of love and passion, peace and joy—it's what I do
Each song remembers when we shared the night here
Me and you . . .

Feeling Free

Every day's an endless dream, it's kind of like the rain
You go inside to miss the wet, but the tapping sound remains
It's like this that dreams are formed, they linger on forever
The one I cherish most of all will never end, no never

So maybe you might understand the way I feel today
My mind and heart are singin' and always seem to say
I want to be free
Free to be me
To find who I am and what I can be
So please come along
Can't someone see
And make a believer out of me

I wish I believed that I'd someday be free
I wish I could break all these chains holding me
I wish I could share all the love in my heart
Remove all the bars that still keep us apart
I wish I could be like a bird in the sky
How sweet it would feel if I found I could fly
I'd soar to the sun and look down at the sea
Then I'd smile cause I know what it means to be free

Fly

I'm living on a one way, dead end street
And I don't know how I got there
My house has a circular driveway
Goin' round and round nowhere
The access road's under construction, detour signs since May
On the other side is a boat without a paddle in the bay
Stuck, down on luck
What-on-earth's left to try?

Fly
Fly
When your road gets rough and your way's not clear
And your wheels fall off and it's hard to steer
And you hurt so bad you can't crawl, walk or drive
Fly
Fly

Holding on don't make you strong
Sometimes ground control is wrong
When nothing on this earth can alter why
Fly!

I'm working in a store open 24/7 with locks on every door
Sales are slim, it's a tile company with carpet on their floor
The rat race won't let me stop for gas
And my car's jammed in reverse
So I walk up hill both ways to work
Cause my only other option is a hearse

Stuck, down on luck
What on earth's left to try?
You see a bigger picture when you're high
Than when you're low
Don't let life's traffic tower keep you down or tell you no

Forever You're My Love

I know I've known you long before we met
A gift to me from the gods of love, then caused us to forget
Our union meant to be decided then by you and me
That we would find each other no regret

You're everything a woman dreams to be
More beautiful and lovely than anyone else to me
You behold things with your soul our eyes have never seen
Our match was made in heaven, fairy tale, a fantasy

This is why I love you
Why I honestly love you
The rhythm of your dance, the way you move creates romance
No one in this world is more amazing
I have always loved you, a blessing from above
Forever you're my lady, forever you're my love

With the perfect look of a porcelain doll you smile
Sophisticated elegance in a subtle sensual style
An angel without wings, ordinary miracles you bring
In you there's peaceful purity no guile

I can't believe you love me like you do
My many imperfections glaring yet your love sees through
You love life's simple pleasures and pamper secret treasures
Your tender touch says more than any words

Yes, I love you
I honestly love you

Give Every Part of All

I know the theory, kissing on the first date's forward, wrong
And holding hands and hugging on the second leads them on
Making out is protocol for third date chemistry
And fourth date's when the love kicks in
That's built on the first three

They say it's just like baseball, first three dates are times at bat
A single, double, triple, safely on base, but just that
For me, this ain't the way to play it, I go for the wall
Always swinging for the fence, cause fans all dig the long ball

When you swing, swing for the fence, so hard you almost fall
When you dance, dance every dance, and go to every ball
When you fight, fight with might, you lose, you still stand tall
And when you love, hold nothing back, give every part of all

I know the theory, when you're swimming, test the water first
When buying cars, you test drive every model, best and worst
In picking schools, you visit several universities
In choosing work, you weigh your option possibilities

But this is why so many never swim or drive nice cars
Or go to school to get dream jobs, now left behind in bars
For me, life's not a dress rehearsal, watching while we wait
It's jumping in and swinging for the fence on every date

It's easier to get forgiveness than permission to play
So go for it right now, cause every now can never stay
Life's a horse race, drop your reins, get out of your stall
Unleash your dog, and let him hunt, give every part of all

Give My Heart to You

Life is a journey with heartbreaks galore
Trust is a luxury I can rarely afford
All that I can hope for is you will give your heart to me

Tears are expensive and I've yet to heal
'Cause words can't cure anything, the soul cannot feel
That's why

All I want to do is give my heart to you
To know you, to show you, to share my soul so true
And all I want from you is to know that you need me
To give you everything is all I want to do

Life has its lessons and I've kept the score
I've been there, I've done that, I don't want no more
I know I had taken your love for granted, but now I am new
Tears are expensive for a heart that won't heal
But I won't turn back now cause this is how I feel
That's why

Every day I worship you every way
Every night I pray till the morning light
You need to know I love you
I love to know you need my love too

Good At What You're Bad At

Here's to the amazing, how fashion's always changing
Like women's bathing suits through history
In the '20s to their ankles, in the '40s to the knee
Now liberated women seldom wear them to the sea

Here's to movements blazing, with icons rearranging
Though faces come and go the protest's loud
Reckless rebels, youth gone wild, against the grain and crowd
Passion pounding renegades, defiant stating proud:

If you be one who will be bad
Be good at what you're bad at
Off the rack in a custom world
Don't care what others scoff at
Fitting in is sin this revolution's not a fad
The words may change but we're still here
Bad means good and good means being
Good at what you're bad at!

Here's to addicts phasing, we're hooked on phonics raging
What once was cool is now be "rad" and "fly"
"Hi" is now "what's up" and "word" replaced the old "no lie"
"Fo fo, no mojo, bling bling is dough" now our reply

Snoop Dog monotone with beat box violence bout they should
Shoes is kicks and hats are lids now represent the hood
Baggies, ridin' low in rides that hop just 'cause they could
A breed with spirits freed who want one thing
That's understood:

Politically correct is out of hand
Won't pacify the status quo and stoop to their demand
Elvis, Lennon, Jerry Lee, Beastie Boys, and AC/DC
Hey, yeah we . . .
We gotta be who we gotta be

Good Intentions Never Do a Thing

Johnny was the smartest kid in every class at school
He learned to read before the other kids learned reading rules
Light skinned, he was sensitive to sunburn out at play
So he bought a lot of lotion, "Bring the sun on," he would say

He practiced kissing in the mirror, love he knew clear through
But all this preparation is intention, less you do

Knowing how to read and never reading seems so wrong
Sunscreen cannot help much if you never put it on
A kiss ain't a kiss, till you give it away
And share the bliss it brings
Good intentions never do a thing!

Julie was a beauty queen, with style and grace, the look
No matter what a man thought, she could read him like a book
Her fair skin, smooth and beautiful, shade from sun was key
She loved the beach yet knew the secrets to stay wrinkle free

By herself, rehearsed her kisses, waiting for love true
But all this preparation is intention, less you do

Good intentions pave the road to broken dreams again
Hell is where the one you are meets who you might have been
Wish I, shoulda, coulda, woulda had what the good life brings
But good intentions never do a thing . . .

Growing Old Together

Today I saw a couple holding withered hands to talk
I saw them snuggle in real close to finish their long walk
Then I saw him open up her door and walk round the car
And she leaned across to open his and kiss her long-time star

Later on I saw them by the pool, beside the gym
Though there were younger, fitter men,
She still had eyes for him
So I asked what their sweet secret was, for lasting, living love
He smiled, it's just one thing young friend
The only thing I think of

We're growing old together, the old man said, can't you see
Then he looked at her so differently
Than the way he looked at me
I wake up to the thought of you, our long-term plan is clear
When others walk away, we stay, forever means from here
Growing old together, day by day, it's destiny
We're growing old together, and the best is yet to be

I looked inside myself and saw a heart that had been used
To the point where my emotions
Had been toyed with and abused
I saw devotion to the notion love was just romance
To the point where my desire burned to take most any chance

And yet in watching this fine pair
Who still played truth or dare
Together fifty years, still dreaming
Planning things they'd share
I asked him what their secret was
To a love I'd never known
He smiled, it's just one thing
Through thick and thin we've grown

Hallelujah Lady

One day my lady came back to me
Her slippin', slidin' ways had fled, lovely as can be
Many dreams I'd just fulfilled
She met me by the sea
Her sunshine smile said
Thanks for love, the best is yet to be

Hallelujah lady!
My oh my she's grown
Hallelujah lady!
She'll never be alone

Trials and tribulations we must all go through
Headaches, heartaches, conscience strikes
They're not just for you
Erase the bad times lady
Make them all a blur
No matter what your past has been
You have a spotless future

You cannot feel a failure without your own consent
So take control you're on a roll
Good times are not yet spent
One last word my lady
Forget about old strife
I like your style, it sparks your smile
Now live a Hallelujah life

Hard to Hear What You Say

Still water runs deep
A quiet man has a lot of things cookin'
Silence can speak
You can see a lot just by lookin'

We need to listen between the lines
And notice all the warning signs
To find what's real, we've gotta feel
Cause feeling's what defines

If you really love me, show me
If you need me, really know me
I'd rather see a preacher live than hear his sermon Sunday
If you really gamble, go me
Cause table talk don't throw me
Actions speak so loud it's hard to hear what you say

Smooth talkin' is cheap
His "what's inside" must match his livin'
Real men will weep
You can gain a lot just by givin'

We need to put intentions aside
And break on through to the doin' side
To find ourselves, we lose ourselves, in service love abides

Walk beside me, don't just point the way
Holding me, says so much more than words could ever say . . .

He Was Doc to Me

Searching for the perfect swing, perfect snow, glassy skiing
Searching while he's gardening, excellence was always king
Always smiling, reconciling work was just to play
He at seventy-nine had lived a lifetime every day

Conquering Olympus peak, rode his bike, was never weak
Conquering he'd always seek, just for fun, no day was bleak
Age meant nothing, always sluffing off how old he was
Strangers soon were friends, every one mattered just because

Who is he, a bird, a plane
Fast as a bullet, a powerful train
Who is he with X-ray eyes
Sees through pain, gives hugs, then cries
Who is he, an *S* in his name
Kryptonite couldn't crimp his game
Who is thin with a big grin, squeezes hands hard cause he can
Who taught tips together, feet apart to share his plan
Who is he, this Superman invincible and free
Some say Don or Papa, but he was always Doc to me

Searching mouths to fix the past
Selling smiles with proud contrast
Searching to dance slow or fast
No one made more card games last
Working, playing Hidden Valley, staying with the best
Soulmates with his Barb, their teamwork better than the rest

War at nineteen, Donald Clyde was captured from the sky
"Non Illegitimate Carborandum," he did cry
Stronger in and out than every other bigger guy
Sansom lived to teach us all
What he had learned and how to fly
Silver Fox, we love you, you will never die . . .

Hero to You

A hero's journey starts with being real
A circle not t'ward having, but becoming as we feel
Then the circle turns toward imagining a dream
Then doing what our mind and heart want, working as a team

But human doings aren't our heroes, human beings are
The circle's not complete until we make our lives the star

I need my life to demand of me, every moment consciously
All my courage, all my strength, all my love to risk at length
I need my life to keep its course, not cause of another force
Just from me who lets it flow
Those who flow as life flows know
I feel no wear, I feel no tear, I need no mending, no repair
There's nowhere to go, if I go with life's flow
There's nothing to do, but serving as a hero to you

I plan, God laughs, me thinking I'm in charge
Believing I can rule my world is thinking small, not large
In a symphony I only play the music there
A single instrument, perform my best to blend, not blare

The hero's journey starts with being all that I can be
But the circle's not complete till I make others more than me

Heroes aren't spectacular in things they do or say
The ones I know live out of sight, transforming life each day
Quietly they flow in every age, in every size
I pray to be among them, Buddha, gaucho wise

How Dirt Poor the Wealthy Are

A wealthy father took his daughter on a country ride
To show her how poor people live
And the shame they have to hide
After two nights on a farm with a family poor as poor
They went back home and Dad asked,
"Can you see why the poor need more?"

"What did you learn from the trip, girl?" as they exited the car
She answered,
"Thanks, Dad, thanks for showing me how poor we are."

"We have one dog, they have four
We buy food, they grow and store
Our pool goes to the garden bend
Theirs is a creek that has no end
We have a small yard
They have fields that go beyond our sight
We have lanterns from Brazil, and they have stars at night
Walls protect us, friends protect them, love is never far
It's amazing how dirt poor the wealthy are."

Now back at the mansion, all their money had no charm
She had servants serving her, but they serve others on the farm
Her deck reached the street
Theirs stretched far as they could see
She played video games while they enjoyed love's company

"What did you learn?" her dad asked, "now comparing us so far"
She answered,
"Thank you, Dad, for showing me how poor we really are."

Have you noticed the richer we get the poorer we are
That happiness is something that dear Wall Street cannot jar
True wealth comes from family, friends
We've got to raise our bar
It's amazing how dirt poor the wealthy are

How Real Country Music's Supposed to Sound

One night I heard a drummer, kickin' up the heat
Then a bass man strapped it on, and matched the beat
Soon a banjo and his fiddle friend thought that they'd sit in
Which caused a pedal steel to cry out for his mandolin
But when the guitars played, I realized what I'd found
This is how real country music's supposed to sound

Yeah, we twang our words and southern drawl our story lines
We're proud blue grass don't mix real well
With sushi and fine wines
We can play that R & B and pop and rock around
But why, when we know
How country music's supposed to sound

You can even add a gospel choir singing praise and love
In country music we are proud of faith in the man above
Throw in thanks to soldiers, waving flags and freedom found
Yes, this is how real country music's supposed to sound

How You Spent Your Dash

(Adapted from the poem "The Dash" by Linda Ellis)

An old man wrinkled in his face and withered in his hands
Died last week at 96, left footprints in our sands
Thousands came to mourn and show respect for a life so fine
His tombstone said 1903 dash 1999

The preacher read his date of birth
And the date of death brought tears
But the part we celebrate, he said
Is the dash between those years
Sure the wealthy man had houses, cars and gobs of cash
But what mattered most was the way
He loved and how he spent his dash

Our dash might only last a while so slow down, watch and feel
Take the time to understand, what's true and all that's real
Treat each other with respect, decide all you would change
Then live your life with the time that's left
While you still can rearrange
So, when your eulogy is read and your actions they rehash
You'll be proud of all the things they say
'Bout how you spent your dash

The old man's life was a testament of service above self
He gave more than he took, selfishness put up on a shelf
The preacher said he never angered
And was very slow to speak
He listened in between the lines
Compassion he would seek.

He loved to live and lived to love
And more often wore a smile
The preacher said he even thought
The homeless had great style
So he said the dash means all the time
You spent alive on earth
And all of you who loved this man
Know what this line is worth

I Am Finally Here, But You're Gone

(Man/Woman Duet)

Man
I packed my bags with guarded feelings, girl
Discarded broken souvenirs
Torn intentions wet with tears
Collected while my memories swirl

If only I had known I'd never see your smile again
I'd shown a different side of me back then

But you're gone
And you don't know what you've got till it's gone
I'd give anything just to have you back
To love for one more day
I'd give anything to hold you
One more night and dance each song away
I miss your kiss and oh, I long, that we could carry on
I am finally here, but you're gone

Woman
I wonder what you're doin' now, my man
You're gone with sadness now a fixture
A thousand words can't paint your picture
Knowing now the reason I ran

With deep regrets I ponder consequences of my past
I should have shared my secrets first and last

Gone but not forgotten, you're the missing piece of we
Gone without forgiving is the reason you left me
Living separate lives is not the answer, we're not free
Knowing what we now know just imagine where we'd be

I Had to Play

I had to play the game today and I had to play it well
I had to make you proud of me, and rise each time I fell
I miss your words of "never quit," won't let you down a day
I'm sorry, coach, I can't stop now, today I had to play

Once there was a young man named Brian and
He was a football star
Today was the biggest game of the year
It was against the archrival school
The winner of the game would be named League Champions
Brian was excited, his coach was too

As the team entered the locker room to dress for the game
An emergency phone call came in to the coach
Brian's father just died
Should the coach wait until after the game to break
The sad news or should he tell Brian now and risk losing?
Brian would surely go home and he was the captain
The team leader, he was needed to win
Well, the coach told him
To his surprise, Brian took the news like a weather report
And simply said, "I'll go right after the game."

Brian played unbelievably awesome
He almost single handedly won the game
As the team left the locker room, the coach approached Brian
Feeling he had taught over-devotion to sports, angrily
He blurted, "Why did you do it Brian? Why did you play? Your
    father is dead. I'm ashamed of you and of myself."

Brian solemnly explained, "I'm a senior
This was my last game
I had to play like I'd never played before.
You see, I love my dad and this is the first time
He'd ever seen me play."

The coach didn't understand. "What do you mean?"
With tears streaming down his cheeks, Brian replied
"You didn't know my father was blind, did you?"

I Love You

I love the way your chestnut hair cascades
And rests on shoulders bare
I love your denim eyes and how they smile
And no way truth disguise
I love your lips and pearly whites
That take a kiss to higher heights
I love your body close to me and how you touch me tenderly

Every moment, every day, all of this and more I mean
Every time I say:

I Love You
I Love You
Just the way you are
All the old, all the new
I Love You

I love the way you notice me
And see the side the world can't see
I love your calm and peaceful way of
Turning pain back into play
I love the way you laugh and cry and
Share emotion on the fly
I love the way you love to give
For God, and family, friends you live

Every moment, every day, all of this and more I mean
Every time I say:

This I promise now for time, and all eternity
Pure devotion, yours forever, by your side I'll be
I'll live for you, I'll fight for you
My loyalty will die for you . . .

Every moment, every day, all of this and more I mean
Every time I say
I Love You

If You Have to Tell Them That You Are, Then You're Not

A famous actor sat back in the corner out of sight
A hundred movies and two Oscars clearly proved his might
The emcee introduced the latest starlets on TV
Yet never mentioned this true legend, he had failed to see

Suddenly a hostess spied him, whispered, "You're the star"
"Don't you feel left out, no one acknowledged who you are?"

He smiled, if you have to *tell* them that you are
Then you are not
Tooting your own horn is like the cowboy with a big hat braggin'
    'bout cows he ain't got
Like a weatherman who thinks he has to tell us when it's hot
If you have to tell them that you are . . . you're not

Two wealthy men each donated a million to the school
One said that a building would be named for him, his rule
The ceremony covered on TV was this man's plan
With not a single mention of the other donor man

Suddenly a trustee recognized this humble star
And asked, "Why you are keeping press
From knowing who you are?"

The great ones quietly will strengthen, softly flex their might
The toughest, baddest dudes we know
They never have to fight
Giving, doing when you'll never get the credit due
Is the loving form of living, private victory sees you through

Knock Down Get Up Man

I've been burned and shaken
Had my lawn mowed, flooded tears
Some call them acts of God, I call them growing years
Been shot down at a dance club
And left like a broken winged dove
Flyin' round in circles never ever finding love

Had train wrecks on the weekends and credit cards declined
Even blown a tire late at night with a spare I couldn't find
Been taken downtown for some barroom brawls others began
I guess you'd call me a knock down get up man

Life's a title fight
You get knocked down, get up again
You can lay there eight counts
Just be on your feet by ten
Rocky fought the odds and Rambo lived because he can
Won't die before I'm dead
I'm a knock down get up man!

My heart's been broken many times
Then smashed again to sand
Can't tell you why, the girls don't cry
I'm king of one night stands
I've lost my job, been downsized twice, never been a CEO
Tried suckin' up to bigwigs, but didn't make more dough

Spilled drinks on tables, tracked in mud
Been late I can't tell time
Been bucked off broncos, kicked by bulls
Never won a rodeo dime
I've hit the wall going way too fast like NASCAR drivers can
Though young, I'm old man wise
I'm a knock down get up man!

I've Fallen in Love with You

You smiled at me and had me at hello
We talked, you shared the things I yearned to know
We danced and held each other tight and so
We cuddled, kissed, let inhibitions go

And I knew
I couldn't fight the feeling flowing through
I've waited all my life, it's true
And now there's nothing I can do
I've fallen in love with you

One night turned to months it's still the same
Love at first sight sparks are now a flame
We're friends forever playing passion's game
What we started will never have a name

I love the way your eyes smile every time you look at me
I love the way you comfort through my insecurity
I love the way you touch me and your tender honesty
The night we met you started to complete me

Keep on Swinging

At a baseball game, the same guy struck out
Three times in a row
In fact he hadn't had a hit since seven games ago
In the final inning, bases loaded, two outs, he's at bat
The coach called time out, walked out to home plate
To have a chat

He said it's not the slump you're in that defines you today
It's what you hope to become and facing
What's now in your way
If he throws it hard or changes up don't lose your nerve
Like the road of life, a corner's not the end, it's just a curve

Yeah a broken clock is right twice a day
Never give up, it's the only price that everyone can pay
No matter what your past has been, your future starts today
To get out of a slump, you gotta keep on swinging
Until you find a way

The pitcher wound up, threw high heat
He swung and missed again
Then strike two, then a ball that nearly hit him in the chin
But he got up, brushed himself off, grabbed his bat
And stared him down
Then pointed at the fence to say
The next pitch he would pound

The pitcher wound up one more time to finish off the game
But he hadn't heard the coach's word
And that the batter thought the same
The pitch, the swing, he hit a home run farther than just far
It cleared the stadium and hit the pitcher's brand new car

Keep on swinging, that's the key
In ten times up to bat the superstars only hit three

Kelly Can Dance

Kelly is so beautiful, to me
Everything that's wonderful, in her you can see
She illuminates the ordinary with her smile
She consumes each moment with extraordinary style
Loving just to love, she comprehends romance
And oh yeah, Kelly can dance

Kelly is so beautiful, to me
Everything that's wonderful, in her you can see
She appreciates the simple pleasures in her life
She is love and peacemaker in every toil and strife
Being just to be she plans her steps out in advance
Oh yeah, Kelly can dance

Dance, life's a dance
All the world's a stage we can enhance
Gracefully she feels and moves to lighten others loads
Graciously she's there for those on life's less traveled roads
All her choreography is goodness at a glance
Oh yeah, Kelly can dance

Kelly is so beautiful, to me
Everything that's wonderful, in her you can see
She so advocates for children, strangers call her friend
She is mother dear to four, unselfish till day's end
Serving just to serve, she performs at every chance
Oh yeah, Kelly can dance

Those in tune enough to hear life's music can't sit still
Kelly's song reminds us how to make our living real

Language of the Heart

There's a secret language only lovers know
Following their hearts to places heads can never go
Without a word their lips and hands and want-me eyes reveal
Like dancing partners sensing where to go, they move by feel

Yes the eye's the window to the soul
Lovers look inside and see that passion makes them whole
Lustfully they fantasize about how love should be
Then find a soul mate seeking self-fulfilling prophecy

Language of the heart is never said or written down
Words can't capture what we mean
The silence makes the sound
Spirit talks to spirit through emotion sets apart
The language only lovers know, the language of the heart

There's a secret language only lovers know
Feeling, self-revealing, laying low, and goin' slow
Hearing, tasting, smelling, touching, seeing senses flow
Body talk connecting, only honesty can show

A squeezing one, two, three says I love you
A nod and sultry smile says I am thinking 'bout you too
Touching toes beneath the table's better than dessert
And without public affection is the way real lovers flirt

A tender touch says more than words can say
A kiss heals hurt and sends the pain away
Holding me, like you'll never let me go
Is the reason why I know

Last Cliché

There are lessons from the heart
We should remember as we roam
Like no success can compensate for failure in the home
Another teaches broken clocks are still right twice a day
So don't give up on anyone, God makes no junk they say

You can't increase a man's performance making him feel bad
Failure's not a person, its events that make you sad
No matter what your past has been you have a spotless future
Live and let live, laugh and love, forgiveness you must nurture

I know you've heard these catchy quotes at work and play
And you're busy complicating life, so blow off what they say
But when lessons learned are lost and you can't find your way
There's always hope for holding on
Until you're down to your last cliché

We don't care about storms but did you bring in the ship
If you're burned out it's okay cause at one time you were lit
If you're defined by what you do instead of who you are
You're just a human doing, not a human being star

Nuggets of pure wisdom, in a rhythm when they're told
Cutting through the clutter, good clichés expose the gold
Sage's lectures for the ages, teaching right from wrong
And the best part is they're usually one line long . . .

Last Time I Ever See Me

When you came into my life you made me real
Around you I can't masquerade, behind my mask to feel
You bring out the goodness from my soul
Tearing down my walls with love, trust is on a roll

Through our honesty, you make me be who I gotta be
So please don't ever leave
Or it will be the last time I see me

If you leave it'll be the last time I see me
The last time I'll be crazy in love
Can't you see without you I'll just be a memory
So please don't leave, or it'll be the last time I see me

When we talk my layers pull apart and peel
With amazing sensitivity and openness you heal
Every day with you my heart is glad
You are better than any best friend a lover ever had

Through authenticity, when I'm with you I'm always free
So please don't ever leave
Or it will be the last time I see me

People spend their lives just tryin' to find themselves and be
Yet never do, because of who's around them constantly
With you I'm complete, you're the better part of me

Learn the Lesson and It's All Good

As I've lived life, there's no mistakes
There's really only lessons
When you lose, don't lose the lesson
When you pray, don't miss the blessin'
Sometimes things don't happen like we thought they would
Learn the lesson and it's all good

When you win, begin again, improve from repetition
When you fail, don't think to cheat
When you're beat, don't think defeat
Winnings not in points, but giving everything you could
Learn the lesson, and it's all good

The lesson is don't complicate the way we live and feel
The lesson's in the fundamental truths that keep it real
All shades come from three base colors, red and yellow, blue
Only twelve notes in music, look what Elvis did with two
We have just four taste buds, yet each food is understood
Learn the lesson, keep it simple
Learn the lesson, and it's all good

We think twice as many words as we speak in every minute
When you talk, connect beneath it
When you teach, be open in it
Even disagreements bring us close, and yes they should
Learn the lesson, and it's all good

Let's Dance

Man
When she walked in I knew she'd been the lady in my dreams
I'd been around the block, but love will find her way it seems

Can she see I want her in my arms
Wrapped in body language charms
Hearts pressed, pounding to the beat, it's right
Aphrodite, god of Love, hook me up tonight

Woman
I caught his eye and knew then what I'd come in here to do
Been lookin' for love in all the wrong places, now my search was
    through

Can he tell I want him to want me,
Snuggled in deep fantasy
Caressing, lust confessing, unashamed of who may see
He's from my dreams, Aphrodite, lead us home to thee

Let's dance
Cheek to cheek
Slowly grooving
Shhhhh, don't speak
One dance to give romance a chance
Senses at their peak

Let's dance
Hold me like you'll never let me go
Cuddle close, trust we show, movin' as our feelings flow
Whisper "I'm so beautiful"
Take my breath away
I am yours and you are mine, when we softly say
Let's dance

Life Is a Long Country Road

To get to Grandpa's house you've got to take the highway south
Then turn off onto Deer Creek Road and drive
It's steep and dusty, rocky with a rut six inches deep
When you get there you're just glad that you're alive

But, Grandpa always laughs and says his road is just like life
Don't get into a rut, it's tough to steer
Just hold on with both hands and stay on higher ground you'll see
Though out of sight, your destination's clear

No one said that life would be a smooth path from your door
With perfect weather every day and a sale at every store
No there's no express lane or a way around wide loads
Life is a long country road

Driving back from Grandpa's for the thousandth time it seemed
I reminisced on all our memories shared
Fishing—catching nothing; hunting—never seeing deer
It's not the destination, it's the journey he declared

Winding turns with ups and downs, I knew the road by heart
Though rough I took for granted it's okay
Suddenly I hit a bump that wasn't there before
Skidding, I recovered thinking what would Grandpa say

Grandpa said if you start your trip with the end in mind you'll see
No matter what may happen 'long the way there's just one key
It's all about the road you're on—the right road, don't pretend
Not a race or competition, only driving till the end

Livin' a Lifetime Every Day

I don't know where I'm going, but I'm making real good time
A motivated mass of indirection in my prime
You think I am lost 'cause I'm not what you thought I'd be
But being you will hold me back and slow down finding me

They say your future's never found while living in your past
So I accelerate my day and make my memories fast

Go—Go—Goin' my way
I'm takin' my soul where my mind goes to play
Go—Go—Goin' my way
I'm livin' a lifetime every day

I can't help getting older, but I don't have to get old
A pampered classic car is worth more now than when it sold
I'd rather die while climbing up than at the mountain's base
So I speed, 'cause the view don't change if I'm in second place

Yeah, I ride unbridled, bareback, wild and fancy free
I hurry up to wait, but fast and furious is me

I eat my dessert before my main course every meal
Burn my candles at both ends, more time I'm tryin' to steal
Wear a black tuxedo in a brown shoe world that's lame
You laugh 'cause I'm different, I laugh cause you're the same

Look North for You

(Sung by a woman)

I'm livin' life from end to beginning, oh what could have been
Slipping into our past love and the touch of your sweet skin
Summer passion, down by Fillmore, shared what love's about
But haven't heard a word since you drove north and I drove south

Love notes, poems, and promises we made, I still recall
All the ways we were, I know for sure, we had it all
So on those long and lonely drives, living separate lives
and wondering if you miss me too
I stop just past Fillmore and look north for you

I've settled down with family, but my heart don't understand
I'm torn between two lovers, one a memory, one a man
Left to live in limbo, haunted by your love and how
You never wrote or called since you drove north and I drove south

Looking north is nothing new, a compass points that way
Looking north, it's easy to find south, or so they say
You can't live in the past, but can let a little live in you
I wonder what you're doin', are you ever lookin' too . . .

Look, Touch, Kiss

Woman
I caught you undressing me with a shy, sly, sultry glance
Flirting peek-a-boo across the floor, your game of chance

Man
Holding hands, they take turns talking and whisper to my heart
Throbbing, squeezing, they won't come apart

Woman
Tangled in each other's arms the music stops and so

Man
Passion pleads we'll find a way to say more than hello

Oh oo oh, three things now we lovers know
Making love with just a look is fantasizing bliss
Talking with a touch, there are no deeper words than this
And slowly sliding towards each other's trembling wetted lips
It's all about the look, the touch, and the anticipated kiss

Man
Night life now is over, at your door, will you be mine
Your want-me eyes, you can't disguise, give silent, subtle signs

Woman
Cuddling, caressing cheek to cheek, you take my hand
With fingers intertwined we understand

Man
Fantasies still steaming, time to go, you hold me tight

Woman
But our time won't be complete without that magic kiss goodnight

Imagination makes our senses feel more than we see
Without a sound we wonder what could happen, what will be
So let all inhibitions go, and body talk to me . . .

Looks Like Heaven While She's Raising Hell

Angel is a prim and proper lady
Manners rare, with perfect hair, won't ever let it down
Outside actions never have been shady
A snobbish prude, so straight it's crude, each day out on the town

But when the sun goes down
Somehow her moon and stars collide
'Cause in the darkness Angel Jekyll
Turns to hellish Hyde

Angel Jekyll and Hellish Hyde, two girls known so well
In the day she looks like heaven, at night she's raising hell
Private riot, wild, she'll try it, quiet kisses says don't tell
Daytime Angel, nighttime devil
Looks like heaven while she's raising hell

Outside she's aloof and keeps her distance
Always by the rules, she stays in bounds, between the lines
Outside temptings always meet resistance
A prissy pure perfectionist, temptation she declines

But when the sun goes down her squeaky cleanness is denied
'Cause in the darkness Angel Jekyll turns to Hellish Hyde

Inside, outside, devil, angel
Swinging, swapping, heaven or hell
What's your mood, you pick and choose
Either, or, you cannot lose . . .

Losers Make God Cry

The native legend, so it's said, is life is short then long time dead
Sixty to a hundred years is nothing to what lies ahead
Yet what we do from A to Zed, the many things our souls we've fed
Determine if we end our lives, in the black or in the red

Life's too short, not fair, they've plead, for those who died before
    they're dead
They spent their time dreaming in bed, and never worked to get
    ahead
They're negative from foot to head, they never live, complain instead

Losers,
Life abusers
Confusers of the reason why, we're here on earth to win then die
Not to beat another, but to better our own high
Refusers to comply they have their wings yet never fly
Losers make the devil happy
Losers make God cry

Losing doesn't mean to lose a race against the clock or crowd
It means you quit before it's through or never race for fear, too
    proud
It's falling down and staying there when you could rise to cheers so
    loud
And pointing fingers for our failures blaming sunlight or a cloud

We are children of the universe called here and now
Supposed to be on earth today, a pre-existent vow
God won't force us heavenward, yet still the losers lose somehow

Loss into a Gain

Attendees filled the ballroom searching for new answer light
When what they really needed was the right answers still right
The speaker said think outside lines, don't close your mind with
    locks
But what if life's true answers are still here inside the box

A broken clock is right twice every day
God makes no junk, you're here for a reason, stay
You're never beat until you quit your views
Bad score, no, time ran out but you didn't lose
Pain is a sign to grow not cry, and once we learn the lesson pain is
    teaching and the why
The pain will go away and won't remain
Just five simple solutions that turn loss into a gain

A package came, you opened it, a complex techno mess
Yet following instructions, the assembly was your best
And so it is in life, at first it's hard, you think you'll fail
And if you do, it's no big deal, there's reason to prevail

When you're sophisticated, yet your life gets complicated, and your
    hope seems confiscated down the drain
The cure for life's contusions, that will heal your mind delusions, are
    just five simple solutions oh so plain

Love Me Still Tomorrow

If you only knew the feeling I get when I'm near you
If you only knew the reason I do the things I do
If you only knew the thoughts I think and what I want to say
You'd love me still tomorrow and not just for today

Your hair, your eyes, your smiling face reminds me of my dreams
Your tender touch and awesome ways I've always known it seems
Your casual calm right from a psalm makes me want to say
Please love me still tomorrow and not just for today

We've only known each other in such a simple way
But you turned my flicker to a flame, so listen when I say
Please love me still tomorrow and not just for today

I've often wondered what it's like to fall in love so soon
Relations usually take some time beneath the midnight moon
I do believe in you my friend, so take my hand and say
And love me still tomorrow and not just for today
Please love me still tomorrow and not just for today

Love of My Life

I am at the crossroads of my life
The fifty yard line, center court
The best seat in the house to see the game as man and wife
In each direction, no rejection
Only open arms from you, the purest picture of perfection
You are the love of my life

You're my eyes when I won't see
My real when I'm not fully me
My true north every starless night
When lost at sea my beacon light
When broken dreams cut like a knife
You heal my heart and soothe my strife . . .
You are the love of my life

I'm sitting on the beach at the bay
Watching low tide water smooth
Turn into high tide waves and back to smooth all in a day
Like resurrection with affection
You forgive and help me through your constant caring, kind,
    connection
You are love in every way

No matter where I go you're always there
Inside out you know my soul
After all these years we're quite the pair . . .

Love

Love can never be spoken
Love can never be said
Love can never be captured in words outside your head

Oh, it must remain just a feeling, emotion between me and you
Sometimes it's just for a moment or lasts eternally through

To love and be loved is all one needs in life
To feel that you're the only one relieves your sorrow and strife
To know that someone cares enough to sacrifice for you
Makes life a little easier, when you know somebody loves you

Love is a song in a woman
That sings to the heart of a man
Life's full of chances to listen
The sounds say love, yes, you can

A powerful force molding nature
It brings out the sunshine and rain
Life's little hassles are mended
With love life just ain't the same

Love is for all the lonely people
Those thinking love is spelled with *I*
Oh, when you're missing the friendships and lovers
Try givin', give love and fly

Make Me Crazy

(Man/Woman Duet)

Woman
When you look into my eyes I fantasize of what's in store
When you touch my hand I understand what hands are really for
When you kiss me and caress, you take me places I've not been
When you whisper, "I'm your baby," I'm in heaven

When you smile and take a while, to tease me playfully
I can't contain, I go insane and need to give you all of me

Oh oo oh, you make me crazy
Mentally irregular, my limbs go lazy, eyes a blur
Crazy, oh you make me crazy

Man
When you look at me and let me look at you I come alive
When you wrap your arms around me, waiting never can survive
When you move and groove your body, it brews hot intensity
When you breathe, I cop a plea, insanity

When you say you love the way I love, it blows my mind
Hallucination high, brain damage of a sensual kind

You're the, reason I can't think straight
Getting over you, it's too late
Can't control myself, this whole obsession's here to stay,
Don't let the men in white take me away . . .

Oh oo oh, you make me crazy
Mentally irregular, my limbs go lazy, eyes a blur
Crazy, oh you make me crazy

Makin' Memories

So long
It's time to say good-bye
It's time to reminisce on why
I'll miss you all the time and cry so long

The years we shared at play, and lived a lifetime every day
Are history now, it's time to say so long

But we've been makin' memories, makin' memories
I like me best when I'm with you makin' memories
You were my strength to see me through
You were my light when darkness grew
You were my hope, I needed you, makin' memories

So with lonely hearts we sigh
There's no easy way to say good-bye
The time we harmonized won't die, so long
We're friends forever more
If not, then what's forever for?

There were times I wandered helplessly and struggled being me
But because you stood beside me now, our future finds us free
We are climbing through another door, no dream is ever gone
No matter what our past has been, it's time to turn it on

Man I Would Have Been

I was headed down a highway, which way I could not tell
The signs all said to heaven, but that road led straight to hell
I was lookin' for the answers thru the bottom of a glass
But Johnny Walker and Jack Daniels friendships never last

When those boys were running out, you were there for me again
Yeah because of you, I never was the man I would have been

Man I would have been going crazy
Man I would have been full of fright
I would have been a falling star that burned out over night
But like the roll of a winning number, you keep comin' up again
Because of you, I never was the man I would have been

I was married to my habits, but unfaithful to myself
Always chased the mighty dollar, had to be top drawer, top shelf
Yet when that high had bottomed out, you picked me up again
And because of you, I never was, the man I would have been

Thank you for loving me
Thank you for hope
(echo) Something I never knew, until I met you
And thank you for letting me be, and not letting go . . .

Moonlit Maui Night

Cruisin'
How's it, shakka, pidgin play
Jawaiian jams, Kapena singin' "Come Sail Away"
KPOI 93.5 is smoothing Front Street air
Kelly bra, dilemma is rare
(Poo-ohh-koo-knee)

Mount Puukukui standing guard on the bay
Through olden luau island sounds the history will stay
Mala wharf is surfing yet seems anchored to sea
Whales off Kaanapali breach to sing, "Let It Be"

This is heaven, time understands
In paradise the clocks have no hands
Sunrise Haleakala awakens soulful sight
Lahaina sunset steals our breath way in azure light
But nothing can compare, when the spirits let us share
The magnificence of a moonlit Maui night

Chillin'
Hey bra, hangin' loose away
Wialea, kickin' back, where toes and turtles play
In the valley, IAO, the needle saved the day
While Hana's sacred pools heal seven ways

Sugar cane is leaving, Howley's now ride the train
Kona Gold and pineapple so locals remain
Untouched virgin forest, white sand beaches to trod
The simple life preserved here by God

From Molokai to shy Lanai, the night is passion's glove
The Maui moon is magic, it controls the tides of love
Kamehameha sanctified it spiritually entice
There's something 'bout a full moon over paradise

More of a Man

The old grey mare, she ain't what she used to be
Neither is the cow
Home, home on the range ain't what it used to be somehow
The stallion is not studly, hair is falling out, gut rolls
And the rabbits and the roosters have no drive or romance goals

Yes, they're tired, out of shape, yet looking for some kicks
But never fear, the cure is clear, I know the perfect fix

Rub a little Rogaine on their skin while transplants grow
Liposuction, tummy tuck their roly poly dough
Put Viagra in their water till they start to show
Then pacify their midlife crisis, how, I think you know
What, you laugh, absurd you say, won't work, a shallow plan
You're right, and neither will it make a man more of a man!

His wife has changed, she's older and wiser now
Wrinkles here to stay
Looks have rearranged, ain't what he used to see, now grey
Skin cream, color, covers up her age to please her man
Emphasizing how she looks, society's demand

But she's more elegant and charming now than younger chicks
He's the one with problems and how do most men find their fix

To be more of a man requires more than what we see
Insight into duty, honor, trust, humility
Real men cry and listen why through sensitivity
Oh why can't more men be more of a man through honesty

Motown Soul

I love makin' music
Creates moves I cannot hide
Some songs happy, some are sad
An emotional roller coaster ride

I love horses, love my farm
My roots can't be denied
But when Marvin Gaye and Smokey sing
Sensual healing stirs inside

I love Motor City
But Nashville was my goal
That's why my baddest country songs
I sing with Motown soul
I crave the fiddle and love the slide
And a two-step, cotton-eyed stroll
But for you to feel my country songs
I gotta sing with Motown soul

I love country lyrics
'Bout leavin', losin' dreams
When you play the music backwards
You get it all back, more it seems

I love the Grand Ole' Opry
Tradition should abide
But the acts we will remember
Expose a passion deep inside

I can't help myself, if I hold back I'll blow apart
The rhythm makes me crazy, moves my body, grooves my heart
Fast or ballad slow my country songs are never whole
Till something happens when I sing that's out of my control

Never Give Up on Your Dreams

As life goes by, we always search for meaning
And look for love and why we seem to fall
Here we are, not knowing what the future finds
But it's just a matter of time before our rhythm finds a rhyme
Before our bells will start to chime, before we end our uphill climb

You should never give up
You should never give in
Always fight for a brighter tomorrow
When the going gets tough, then the victory begins
No mountain's as high as it seems
So never give up on your dreams

The time will tell if we're not what we seem
If things we do don't match the things we are
So look inside, our happiness is always there
We are simply one of a kind, can't let others make us blind
With some patience we will find, we can do what's on our mind

Work will win when wishing won't
You've got to pay the price
No pain no gain, don't fizzle out
It's time to roll the dice
It's not over till it's over, hang on till the end
You've got to keep the dream alive
You were born to win

Never Told You

(Man/Woman Duet)

Man
I'm the one who wants you
I'm the one who needs you
I'm the one under the sun who truly loves you

Yet here I am so broken hearted
You have disappeared, departed
Fighting back the tears, I can't believe that we're through
You're my everything, this I knew

Woman
I'm the one who knows you
I'm the one who adores you
I'm the one under the sun who's living for you

Yet here I am with my heart guarded
Wishing time could be restarted
Should have shed the fears of showing feelings for you
You're my everything, this I knew

But you never knew I would have been your shelter when it rains on
your parade
Never knew I would have been your comfort when your fire starts
to fade
Never knew I would have been your one and only if I'd followed
through
What would have been, I'll never know, 'cause you never knew
What would have been I'll never know, 'cause I never told you

I'm the one who dreams of you
I'm the one who yearns for you
I'm the one under the sun who now misses you

Man
Yet here I am alone, discarded
Living separate lives, unchartered
Sadness seldom clears, I swear I'd make it with you

Together
You're my everything, this I knew

No One Ever Knows

No one ever knows all that we feel
We live our lives, masquerading
Seldom showing what's real
No one ever knows, everything we want to say
We keep our music stuck inside us
Some notes we never play
And though life's pub is packed with people
We sometimes drink alone
In solitary confinement
Hurting bad to the bone

They say they know what we're going through, our fantasies and
    foes
And know our pleasures and our pains, and what we presuppose
But unless they've stepped and wept through blows
And walked in our shoes highs and lows, No, No . . .
No one ever knows

No one ever knows all we want to be
So we chase the dreams friends find us
Out of fear they'll disagree
No one ever knows the lens through which we see
They tell us this is white and this is green
But they look blue to me
And though in their eyes we're successful
We've died before we're dead
They raped the passion from our purpose
Stole the visions from our head. And still . . .

Everybody hurts sometime
We all have had a nickel when we needed a dime
But you're not me, no sympathy, just give me love that shows
And hold me tight, no words are right, 'cause no one ever knows

No Place Like Home

I'm on the road again, on a steel horse I ride high
Alone again in a crowded room, I laugh so I don't cry
With Junior in my wallet next to little girls with dolls
I keep scribbled notes that say I love you, don't forget to call

A storm begins a brewin', the wind and rain are cold
A victim of the system, chasing dollars sure is old
I'm off to see the wizard, travelin' wide to prove my worth
But Oz is what I leave behind, real happiness on earth

I'm partially the Tin Man, with a heart that beats for you
Part Scarecrow, with a brain recalling all the things you do
I'm Lion, proud, courageous, staying faithfully true
But it's not only in Kansas that I miss you as I roam
It's everywhere, yeah Dorothy's right, there's no place like home

I miss my lovely lady, her eyes, her smile, her smell
Away from you, not in your arms is lonely living hell
To pay the bills and pad our wills and keep the witch away
It's strange I'm on the yellow brick road with munchkins every day

Families are forever, that is what forever's for
Doin' what I do is all for them and what's in store
But the weather's rough and the goin's tough, no Emerald City life
Oz is what I leave behind, my children and my wife.

Not No, Just Not Now

There comes a time in all our lives when cupid flies our way
And shoots his arrows through our hearts to start our Valentine's Day
As kids we want to grow up faster than we should or can
So we overlook the boys our age to find a rugged teenage man

But dating older men before we're sixteen isn't wise
They want things we can't give them, confused in love's disguise
What to do with feelings true when holding hands and kissing's
   through
Save yourself for what's in store, a married love that's so much more

Wait—Love will
I'm worth the wait you'll see
Let's wait—Love will
There's more to us than intimacy
I want you forever, and going slow is how
Wait—it's not no, just not now

I realize we all have needs that surface now and then
The need to hold a good friend and be held by him again
The need to feel affection knowing someone really cares
With heartbeat pounding nervous sounding, breathless times we share

Our dreams are full of knights in shining armor riding free
Who rescue us from loneliness for all the world to see
But better than a macho man who steals my heart and rides away
Is the man who sensitively knows I want to wait and still he stays

Number One

Is there any question, wondering who you are?
Is there ever inhibition, when you try to reach your star?

Do you ever seek the meaning of sometimes why you fall?
Do you ever stop believing that you can have it all?
If this is you, say what I say, don't stall

Oh I believe in myself, 'cause no one else may see
Who I am, and all that I may be
Hang on to a dream among the stars and sun
I whisper, friend, you're number one
(background vocals) You're number one

Have you never seen the writing of successes on your wall
If you've done it once, remember you can again stand tall
If this is you, say what I say, don't stall

Conceive and believe and you will soon achieve
Like an eagle in the sky
Think you can, my man, and reach toward the sun
I whisper, friend, you're number one

Okay, 'Cause You've Got a Friend

I know what's in my garbage could trash my life today
Though put out on the curb, it's never taken all away
I've learned don't cry over anyone who won't cry over you
And the hardest thing is watching who you love, love someone new

But when it hurts to look back and you're scared to look beyond the
    bend
Look beside you, you've got a friend till the end

Everything is okay in the end
If it's not okay, it's really not the end
And if it's not the end, I'll be there until things mend
Everything will be okay,
Okay, 'cause you've got a friend

Falling in and out of love is easy through the years
Love starts with a smile, grows with a kiss, and ends with tears
But friends are like stars, you don't always see them, yet they're there
Like a four leaf clover, hard to find, lucky and rare

So when it hurts to look back and you're scared to look beyond the
    bend
Look beside you, you've got a friend till the end

Friends usually build rainbows, but sometimes they're the rain
And though they caused your tears of pain, they never leave you, why?
They know the only one who can stop your tears
Is the one who made you cry . . .

One in a Billion

They say when you're young
The world is at your feet
To try your best and pass each test and find the peace of mind you seek
And so as you grow, you'll stumble, fall so low
And want to give up times it seems, but never give up on your dreams

You're one in a billion
You're one of a kind
You're one in a billion
Your dreams you will find

I need you to know, live life, take it slow
Don't just talk, but walk the walk, believe, achieve
You can, you know

Only the Elderly Know

Some things are true, whether we believe them or not
Like the old must die, and the young may, no matter how we plot
We won't regret the things we did, just what we didn't do
Getting old and being old are different attitudes

Possessing wealth means nothing, it's the noble use that's great
When much is given, much is now expected, pass your plate
Life, there's no mistakes, there's only lessons to be learned
And only those who've lived enough can teach us and discern

Wisdom is the gift of the elderly
When an old man dies, a library burns to the ground
One old friend is better than two new ones
Slow and steady wins the race, the elderly have found
The power we desire lives within us as we go
These most important things, only the elderly know

Some things are true, whether we believe them or not
Like you'll make a lousy somebody else, be you, don't be bought
It's not having the best players, it's having the right ones
Not what we do, but who we do it with, is why we won

What keeps us alive and well is dreaming mighty dreams
Finding meaning, having purpose matters, so it seems
All we need is to be needed, with good reason to give
And only those who've lived enough, can show us how to live

They say when you lose your dreams you die, so you gotta dream to
    live
Lifelong learners live long lives, they read and laugh and give
Don't you want to die while climbing, not in the valley low
That's why we honor the elderly, 'cause these things they all know . . .

Pebble in the Shoe

The Grand Teton had turned him on each year
Prepared to climb her fourteen thousand feet of fear
He started out determined, to make his dream come true
And no it's not the boulder rocks that made him stop and get the
    blues . . .

It's the pebble in the shoe, yeah the pebble in the shoe
A tiny thing that rubs us raw, till it cuts through
A mighty clock will stop 'cause of one little screw
A rock chip in the windshield will soon crack through
Yeah, David killed Goliath with a slingshot, it's true
With a stone, no bigger
Than a pebble in the shoe

Some sell their 'cedes, 'cause one cheap part breaks down
Some sell their piano, 'cause one key's flat in sound
Some throw the baby out, with the dirty water, true
And no it's not that all is wrong, that causes fools to get blue . . .

They say don't sweat the small stuff, but small stuff is the clue
A baby crawls before he walks and drinks before he chews

Most start their love with vows, and promise they'll stay true
And no it's not the biggest things that break true love in two . . .

Perfect Storm

After work on Wednesday night, I stopped in for a drink
A quiet night, with nothin' goin' on you'd have to think
But don't they say there's always a cool calm before the storm
And outside in the stillness a dark cloud began to form

On the verge of a power surge, you could smell the weather change
And like a hurricane, out goes the sunshine, in comes rain

Lightning struck the door down, thunder rolled me to the floor
She drenched me oh so sensually as her charm soaked to my core
Felt ridden hard and put away wet, then left to dry alone
But it's all good—she's the only perfect storm I've ever known

One year later, Wednesday night, it's after work again
Just chillin to Bob Dylan at our favorite "Do-Drop-In"
They say that lightning never ever strikes the same place twice
Then we heard a bang, the odds had changed, could she have rolled
    her dice
As they all took cover hoping strength they could retain
I cowboyed up to trade my sunshine in for sizzlin' rain

Wham bam, thank you ma'am, her wild waves had their way
Dancin' in her rain is now my favorite place to play
And oh yeah, I'm here it's been a year and it is Wednesday . . .

Quiet Beatle Man

1943 to 0, 0, One
58, lived two lives, died too young
Searching, no more, answers now you see
Meaning of earth madness, finally

Can't believe there's no more songs to come
Yet on the other side I hear there's some
Now with Lennon, Orbison, Hendricks, Elvis, Morrison
Heaven's rock-and-roll band's better now you're there to play
And so are we, 'cause you passed our way

There was something in the way you moved us
In dark times we knew "here comes the sun"
You gave hope and helped us cope, we miss you, every fan
We, with your guitar weep, quiet Beatle man

Liverpool friends, family paved your way
Molded by your music, we're okay
Bangladesh was better 'cause you played
Sitar sounds you fingered all have stayed

With the Fab Four you brought beat new birth
Musically you ministered to earth
Now with Buddy Holly, Joplin, Valence, Skynard, place is hoppin'
Heaven's rock and roll band's better now you're there to play
And so are we, 'cause you passed our way

My sweet Lord you took to number one which set us free
To seek a higher, better way, a love philosophy

Quiet Heroes

The world is full of quiet heroes who never seek the praise
They're always back off in the shadows
They let us have the limelight days
For this you're the one that I look up to
Because of you I'm free
You set an example I could follow
You helped me see my destiny

So even though my thanks don't show
Unnoticed you will never go
I need to say I love you so
You're my hero

I've had my share of broken dreams
But you said I could win
You gave me the chance I always needed to start my dreams again
You took the time to teach and tutor and show me rules to rise
You changed my fears to glory tears
You're an angel in disguise

I wouldn't be where I am today, I've won my share of times
Unless you coached me through the maze and pushed me on the
    hardest climbs
It's just your style, the extra mile, no glory must be tough
You let me have the accolades
A smile, you said, was just enough

Rainbows Only Follow Rain

(Man/Women Duet)

Man
There's a struggle over there, rat race calling, balance rare
Family needs him, games to see, no time off from the company
Wants a raise, needs a life, chasing fame, lost his wife
Stable job, then let go, can't hold on 'cause he doesn't know

No one knows true joy until we face some sorrow
No one knows strong faith until it's tested out
We won't know peace until we're faced with conflict
Or know high hopes until we're filled with doubt
We'll never understand true love until it's lost in pain
Rainbows only follow rain

Woman
There's cancer calling there, medicine, losing hair
Needs to laugh, loves to feel, bitter grudge won't let her heal
Bills are piling, hurt cuts deep, the road ahead seems mighty steep
Wonders why life knocked her low, wants to quit 'cause she doesn't
    know

Pain is a signal to grow not suffer
Once we learn it goes
There's no light without darkness
No holding without letting go

Real Most Incredible You

I've fallen in love with another woman
The lady I married's no longer around
Young, immature, just like me, insecure
Puppy love we had found

I've fallen in love with a different woman
Amazed by her goodness I'm numb
She's comfortable being the person she is
The older she gets, the more like herself she's become

The real you has taught me that love's not a look at each other
    seducing affection
It's standing together, no matter life's weather, and looking
    the same direction
The real you has taught me that love isn't something you have
    but it's something you do
Yes I've fallen in love with another woman
She's the real, most incredible you

I've fallen in love with another woman
She gives more than any around
Her love never ceases, compassion releases
Her selflessness always abounds

Inside, outside, you're love's total sum
The older you get, the more like yourself you've become . . .

Reason to Live

I've been in stormy weather
I've cried because of fears
But the soul would have no rainbows, if the eyes possess no tears
There's always smoke with fire and usually joy with pain
To appreciate the sunshine you've got to have some rain

So, if you're down and troubled, no matter what you do
Don't focus on the thistle, the rose will see you through
And when your life is broken, it's yourself that you need to forgive
There is light at the end of the tunnel
There is always a reason to live

I've had my share of sadness
I've heard my share of cheers
I've fought my way through friendships
But the real ones they last for years
I've fumbled and I failed some, been up, yeah, I've been down
But I learned to soar with eagles, though my feet are on the ground

So don't be afraid of dying
Be afraid you haven't lived
Always rise each time you fall when your back's against the wall
Eliminate your shame
Your dreams you can reclaim

Redneck Shuffle

When I drive a fancy car I duck
Rather be seen in my pickup truck
Wouldn't be caught dead wearing peach and mauve
No Gap clothes, my Wrangler jeans are definitely more suave

Cannot comprehend the whys and hows
Of those who don't know bulls from cows
I can't take rap and heavy metal songs
That slam our women and praise our wrongs

That's why it's time to clear the floor and other music muffle
Crank up the twang, for a country thang
Let's do the Redneck Shuffle

It's not for . . . purple-haired, body piercing, dope smokin', frisbee
    throwin', bike ridin, skateboard jumpin', flag burnin' people,
    'cause we . . .
Pull out chairs, watch the swears, open doors, do our chores,
    treating every lady right,
Fighting for the things that are right

We love NASCAR, football too
Wrestling we'd love to do
Buckin' broncos, hats and boots, mighty proud of rural roots
Macarena, what's this scuffle
Let us do our Redneck Shuffle!

I can't take it when folks beat their child
At the sight of it I go hog wild
And a man who hits a woman should be maimed
Then thrown in prison to be some guy's boyfriend till he's shamed

Won't fear violence in the streets today
That's why I joined the NRA

Will not compromise my moral code
It's duty, honor, country mode

That's why it's time to clear the floor and other music muffle
Crank up the twang for a country thang
Let's do the Redneck Shuffle

Rocketman

(Sung by a woman)

Looking at the starlit summer sky
The Milky Way reminded me of the night I got to fly
I never knew that love could ever be so wild and free
Till he got down with his bad self and launched my fantasy

Ten, nine, eight, seven, six, five, four
Ignition, trembling, passions roar
Three, two, one, lift off, we're churning, after burning more
Through the stars, past moon and Mars, Nirvana's overrated
Oh, oh, coming with him through the clouds, God's heavens
    overstated
Constantly, relentlessly, he loves me till we land
Oh baby . . . he's my rocketman

My horoscope and tarots failed to show
That I was worthy of a night where every feeling flowed
I never thought I could escape the world in which I live
Until he counted down and pushed my buttons just to give

Rocketman, his mission is to turn me on
Rocketman, he goes where no one else has gone
Equipped and tooled, he's now refueled, with only one flight plan
To take me on another ride, 'cause he's my rocketman

Second Chance

(Man/Woman Duet)

Man
A lonely lady's crying, her heartbeat fades away
Cannot comprehend the hurt she battles every day
Her love once bright and blissful, but passion turned to pain
Her heartbreak hope is rainbows follow rain

Woman
A melancholy man sighs, his heartbeat torn in two
Doesn't understand his mixed emotions bleeding blue
His soul sowed selfless service, support soon slipped away
His heartbreak hope is darkness turns to day

When a broken-hearted woman meets a broken-hearted man
Alone they were lost and lonely, together they know they can
They dance, romance, and take a stance
All in the name of a second chance
Their love once more begun
Two broken hearts can beat again as one

Man
A new dawn meets the morning, all yesterdays erase
Now neatly nestled in each other's loving, warm embrace

Woman
As seasons change and rearrange, we fall then spring to form
Together they can weather any storm

There is thick and thin we know, but never stay unless you grow
Strength comes not from holding on—sometimes it's letting go

Shall We Dance

Dance is a vertical expression of a horizontal fantasy
Rhythmic fluid motions making love in harmony
Passion thick, seduction quick, your hands mold me like clay
Having your way with me, you dominate my sense of play

Twirling, swirling, pas de deux, you set my soul on fire
Then fan my flames and let me burn, releasing all desire
So close I hear you breathe, I feel your heart beat through your sweat
Cheek to cheek you show me reasons why our bodies met

Lost in lust, your moves to music throw me in a trance
And it's all because you whispered, shall we dance

Shall we dance . . .
Let our bodies talk and take us places words can't
Shall we dance . . .
Privately in public every song can stir romance
And it's all because you whispered, shall we dance

Dance is a vertical expression of a horizontal fantasy
Exploring every body curve and possibility
Taking me your hostage I surrender all my shame
Every move you make is dangerous, no chance you'll be tamed

Tangled in emotion you bring out the bad in me
Reckless, dirty dancing in wild choreography
Emancipating every sensual feeling stuck inside
In your grasp I'm safe expressing how my manners lied

All night we've salsa'd in Cancun and waltzed in Paris, France
And it's all because you whispered, shall we dance

She Is Now Wherever We Are

The little soul was born to make things right
Together mom and little girl held on to fight the fight
Days turned into weeks, intensive care for baby Jane
Dad caught word, divorce absurd, came back to ease the pain

Weeks turned into months, a birthday celebration day
And all the other patients brought their gifts to give away
One a smile, another hope, another laughs to help her cope
One brought hugs, another love, and many faith in God above

Then suddenly, sweet baby Jane looked up at the skylight dome
She said, "I'm ready," kissed her mom, reached up, and headed home

The good will always live their total time God set, no more
Some a long time, some a short time, all pass through the door
She's not gone, although no longer where she was, not far
She is now, wherever we are. She is now, wherever we are

Only here for one short year's not fair
But oh the things Jane taught the world, remarkable and rare
Patience, tolerance, forgiving others for their weakness
Loving unconditional, humility, and meekness

Just a year with cheers and tears, but got to know each other
Her life and love revealed what matters most to dad and mother
Families are forever, here to find out who they are
We're only here for a little while, then gone, but never far

Show and Tell

How can I tell you, oh where do I start
The passion I feel in every beat of my heart
Oh how can I tell you, the love that's inside
I want you, I need you, in you I confide

You're everything I hoped for, you're all that I dream
My knight in shining armor, the captain of my team
My beauty queen from a movie scene, my lady luck to go
I really love you baby, but how will you know?

Show and tell
More than say—I must show
Show and tell
It's the way feelings flow
Show and tell
The only way true love will grow
Show and tell—tell and show

How can I tell you, oh where do I begin
The pure joy you bring me, completeness within
Oh how can I tell you, the part that you play
I'm half-whole without you, you strengthen my way

You're everything I want in a woman to be
A sensual feeling, assertive and free
A mind and an elegance, grace and a glow
I really need you baby, but how will you know?

Six S's Everything

(Man/Woman Duet)

Man
There's somethin' bout the way you are tonight
Provocative perfection, an intoxicating sight
Sophisticated elegance, six S's in your file
Smart, Sassy, Sexy, Sensual, Sense of Humor, Style

Smart, you hold your own in every conversation flow
Sassy, when asked how you're doin', asks who wants to know
Sexy, in the way you stand and walk and talk and kiss
Sensual, in the way your passion moves each day to bliss
Sense of Humor, makes me laugh, your smile stops every sting
And Style, you're spiritual and true—six S's everything!

Woman
When you walked in, the room stopped, eyes on you
Who is he, they asked, what does he do
Your total class and polished presence makes you stand alone
It's clear you have six S's unlike anyone I've known

Smart, Sassy, Sexy, Sensual, Sense of Humor, Style it's true
Everything love needs is found in everything in you
Body, mind, and spirit, three dimensional you bring
Six S's yeah—you are everything . . .

Sleep on a Windy Night

A young man came a calling, he was answering the ad
The farmer needed hired help, so he promised all he had
The farmer asked, "Why hire you?" He said, "I'll do what's right,
You'll never have to worry, I can sleep on a windy night"

Late that evening clouds rolled in, disaster dead ahead
The farmer called the lad for help but he was fast asleep in bed
He raced out but the gates were tied, the yard was fastened tight
Everything secure and safe and sound till morning light
Now the farmer knew what he meant, "I can sleep on a windy night"

You can sleep through the night, if inside your skies are blue
Takin' care of business before business takes you
No matter what the forecast, if prepared there's no fright
While others wake and worry
You can sleep on a windy night

A traveling man was lonely left his room to get a drink
She caught his eye and flashed some thigh, his flesh began to think
A storm was raging, lust was caging him in squeezing tight
But he didn't stay, with his wife away, he'd sleep on a windy night

Back at home with kids tucked in, the weather turned real bad
The frightened children climbed in bed and snuggled up to dad
"Will the house blow down, or did the builder build it right?"
Everything secure and safe and sound till morning light
He said, "I am the carpenter, you can sleep on a windy night"

Special Man

A little boy wants to be like his dad
So he watches us night and day
He mimics our moves and weighs our words
He steps in our steps all the way

He's sculpting a life we're the model for
He'll follow us happy or sad
And his future depends on example set
'Cause the little boy wants to be just like his dad

A special man talks by example
Takes the time to play and hug his lad
A special man walks by example
The very best friend a growing boy ever had
Any male can be a father
But it takes a special man to be a dad

He needs a hero to emulate
He breathes "I believe in you"
Would we have him see everything we see
And have him do what we do?

When we see the reverence that sparkles and shines
In the worshipping eyes of our lad
Will we be at peace if his dreams come true
And he grows up to be just like his dad

Stayed to Help 'Em Cry

Mother told her angel to come straight from school
Thirty minutes late, mom lost her cool
Where she'd been? Her friend dropped her doll
Broken pieces and hurt from her fall
So she stayed to help her pick it up, give fixing it a try?
No, she couldn't fix the doll . . .
She just stayed to help her cry

Two brothers talking 'bout their dreams of ball
One signed, one never got the call
Went to visit, gamer blew his knee
Broken hearted after surgery
So he stayed to tell him, cowboy up, get over it, you tried
No, he knew being a man meant
He could help him cry

We can pretend to care
But we can't pretend to be there
We can write or say
But sometimes words get in the way
I believe in love, the silent language of the heart we can't deny
That's why when someone needs you, just hold 'em close and stay
To help 'em cry

Picture perfect family, usually smiling
But now their only daughter's slowly dying
Dignified in her hoops and heels
While in pain, asked how we feel
When she passed away we felt her close,
Though gone she didn't die
Comfort came from God . . .
But she stayed to help us cry

Still Holding On

People come, people go, some you like, some you love
Some you never want to know

Friends and lovers, some will be, some fair weather, some around
For some small specialty

But in a thousand years, a million miles, a billion souls
We only need one, one and only, one who makes us whole

Nobody wants to be lonely
And it's not just the lonely only
Who need to be needed, feel love when defeated
Reminded they really belong
When things go wrong, and everyone else is gone
You're my one and only, the only one still holding on

People come, people go, some you miss, some you don't
Based on memories long ago

Friends and lovers, some will be, satisfying urges with
No lasting chemistry

But in a thousand years, a million miles, a billion souls
We only need one, one and only, one who makes us whole

You have always been for me
Consistently, true loyalty
Loving unconditionally
The answer to a lover's plea, cause

Still You Love

I'm not worthy of your love
Still you love
Not capable of reaching what's expected from above
Falling short potentially, procrastinating endlessly
Others giving up on me
Still you love

Love,
Only known by those in tune with heaven
Love, forgiving seventy times seven
Unconditional, unfeigned, nonjudgmental, no refrain
Only angels understand the meaning of true love
Like blistered, weathered hands that can't go on without a glove
In my sun and rain, still you love

I do not deserve your love
Still you love
Not in your league or the portrait of perfection you dream of
Showing off cosmetically, 'cause underneath I'm scared of me
Even though my real you see
Still, you, love

Still, continues now forever more
You, like no other that's for sure
Love, connected at the core
On your wings, you lift me up to soar above
No matter what, still you love . . .

Stop the Mind Games

When will you come back to me?
I need you oh so desperately
Will you ever pardon me?
And think about the love we shared

I know the foolish games we played
The times I walked away but should have stayed
Actin' hard I thought I had it made
Now you're gone, I've got to declare

Stop the mind games, let's stop the mind games
Don't play with tender hearts, they wither like a rose
Stop the mind games, gotta stop the line games
We both need honesty, so share your soul with me, my love

I hope it's not too late to show
Feelings bottled up you don't yet know
Pride got in the way, our only foe
We had so much, don't throw it all away

I've still got you upon my wall
Cryin' nights, please return my call
We've gotta talk and postpone the stall
Until we do, please hear what I say

You gotta believe that we can make it
You've gotta believe in love
You gotta believe our lines can't fake it,
With verbal push and shove
We gotta remember lovers last when lovers learn to like
Forget the past, the games can't last
Let's start anew tonight

Successify

Slowly cruisin', chillin' out, nothin' goin' on
Wasting away in never land, never right, never wrong
Take no chances, never risk, no rewards or rules
There's no hurry, don't you worry, "oh-whatever's" cool

Losers like this on life's dole, who never sweat or stir their soul
Who put off living won't comply, let's spell it out, successify!

S-U-C-C-E-S-S-I-F-Y, yeah successify
Get off your procrastinator, time's not leased or lent
If you do what you did, you'll still get what you got
And your get up and go just plum got up and went
It's not what's on you, it's what's in you
Not what *you* drive, what drives you
S-U-C-C-E-S-S-I-F-Y, yeah successify

Caught up in society's judgments, cannot win enough
Too afraid of failing, won't attempt, to lose is rough
So they sit there on their heels, and never live, just spin their wheels
They are dead before they die, their only hope, Successify!

We can't just get all that we want, we must want all we get
Life is not a competition, beating others, deep in debt
We are born to be successful, on the wings of dreams we fly
Livin' large and representing starts when we successify!

Sweet Liberty

I need to share a love affair 'bout a lady in my life
She's always there, her beauty rare, a stalwart strength in strife
A knight in shining armor, she stands so proud to see
Defending God's great plan for man, to be all we can be

She says: "Give me your tired, give me your poor
No matter what your race or creed"
Her flame's burning bright lighting freedom's door
A symbol of our destiny
To some she's just a lady, but to me she's my Sweet Liberty

I've been alone with her at night, as she lights the harbor sky
I've watched her pray for peace each day, hand, torch held high
She whispers words of love and hope, and faith that free we'll be
Why can't the whole world listen in and live in harmony

She welcomes in the hungry child, the homeless helpless friend
They come to her with yearning hearts, their huddled masses blend
She teaches justice is for all, a brother, sister plan
She's there to keep life's dream alive for the family of man

Take Time

Time, enough hours to fill all desire and need
There's more to life than increasing its speed
We should smell all the flowers both roses and weed
Life's meaning we'll discover

Time, on a hamster's wheel, goin' round and round
In a rat race game of lost and found
The stuff life's made of can't compound
From one day to another

So take time to work, it's the price of success
Take time to play—the secret of youth is omitting our stress
Take time to read, our source to what's out there
Take time to love and be loved so we all care
Take time to think and laugh and cry and dream that you can fly
'Cause dreams live in our minds and hearts, and only there they die

Time, abide with me tis ev'n tide today
What time is it? It's right now found in clay
I can sculpt it, massage it, and mold it my way
Takin' charge and makin' me

Time, not a haunting past or a future vow
To petty pressures I never will bow
Failure's my friend through the trenches I'll plow
Not control, but flowin' free

The Best Is Yet to Be

There's a time in our living when we rise up when we fall
There's a time in our giving when our courage seems to stall
There's a time when we push ourselves and a time when we give in
For some their dreams and visions take
For some they don't begin

Go for it now, seek the stars, step by step you'll see
Dreams come true to the one who hangs
The best is yet to be
So go for it now, seek the stars, step by step you'll see
Dreams come true to the one who hangs
The best is yet to be

Don't ever give up on your dreams
When you lose your dreams you die
Don't ever give up on yourself, won't feel that natural high
There's a way to fly beyond today, there's a way to conquer fear
Just do today all that you may
Victory's oh, so near

The Bridge

I tumbled off the edge of life and skidded to a stop
Rock bottom, dirty, scraped, and sore, so low I couldn't see the top
The rivers' waves were close at hand, life's rapids raging war
The fog too thick to find my way, stoned blind to what I'm looking for

A stumbling 'long the rocky shore, not knowing how to cope
My heart was torn, my soul in knots, there had to be some hope
Then somehow, some way through the fog I wandered up a ridge
And high above these troubled waters stood a mighty bridge

The bridge is strong and straight and true
No matter what I've done or do
Across the gap I'm homeward bound
I finally walk on higher ground
Was lost, but by the grace of the bridge, I'm saved and safe and sound

Proceeding down the path of least resistance, life was fun
Forgetting spills and seeking thrills, still reckless, wild and on the
    run
Invincible and fancy free, thought all I need is me
I didn't sense the warning signs, was numb to what should be

The dead-end street I traveled on was suddenly not there
I'd fallen off the deep end once again into despair
But somehow, some way in the fall I hit the same old ridge
And found no matter what my past had been, there stood the bridge

I was blind but now I see
That if I can't find the bridge
The bridge has not moved, it's just me

The Main Thing

(Man/Woman Duet)

Man
As they say, you had me at hello
When our eyes met, I just knew you'd know
Woman
You were a familiar song I sing
Instantly our twain was one main thing

Man
You're my *main* squeeze, main frame, main tease,
main-line drug of choice, yes you please
Woman
You're my *main* man, main switch, main fan, mainly
managing our love plan
Together
Chances are, our chances are we will always schwing
'Cause the *main* thing is to make the main thing the main thing

Woman
Everything I am is 'cause of you
No one makes me feel the way you do
Man
I'm your puppet, you control my string
I am me because of one main thing

You've been like a bee buzzing around my mind since I've known me
Constantly obsessed with you my heart has stalked you endlessly
We are proof that matches made in heaven are no fantasy
We are better when together, 'cause the main thing's you and me

The Sickness Made Me Well

A rich man lay there dying, but couldn't buy one more day
It was the wrong thing to be wrong about, a painful price to pay
He's lived his life lookin' through the bottom of a glass for way too
    long
And told me I should change my ways, confess that I was wrong

I am president of a club I didn't want to join
Identity just Johnny C, no dues, don't need no coin
Rich man, poor man members, step by step, just day by day
Thanks to them, I'm glad I finally got the guts to say

I'm sick and tired, being sick and tired
I hit rock bottom, tired being wired
Though sick and off the deep end, down and out I tripped and fell
Thank God, I went through hell . . .
'Cause it was the sickness that made me well

I was king of killing time, forgotten lives, my shame
Being gone is gone, through drink or work it's still the same
I should have been a family man, but no one called my bluff
I pray I still have time to make it up

The Simple Life

Look around,
A motivated mass of indirection,
A rat race 'bout acceleration
Complicated 'cause we think it's a competition game
No, the simple life comes not from fitting in for fear of shame
You laugh 'cause I'm different, I laugh 'cause you're still the same

Life's not measured by the number of breaths we will take each day
It's measured by the number of moments that take our breath away
Feed the hungry it makes us full; Lead, it's harder to push than pull
One can give and never love, but none can love and never give
It's not telling time, but building clocks so those who follow better live
Laugh and cry each day—serve, forgive, it takes away the strife
Make the world a better place— it's the simple life.

Look around,
A constant yearning want from indecision,
A grass is greener there condition
Complicated 'cause we think it's what we have and do
No, the simple life is feeling, flowing, here's the clue
We'd take afternoon siestas if we only knew

Mirror, mirror, what's it all about?
It's being in the moment, being simple every way . . .

Things You Cannot Buy

The TV blabs buy this and that if you want to be cool
The brochures boast go here and there and sunbathe by the pool
The neighbors cry keep up with Jones's, in debt till you die
But where's the show that let's us know 'bout things you cannot buy

Commercials claim this truck and that car always get the girls
The sales pitch for romance is always diamonds, gold, and pearls
The fashion magazines say overweight won't catch an eye
But where's the store for heart and core with things you cannot buy

Money can't buy me love—money can't buy you me
Money can't buy my trust or other traits you cannot see
You've all things that money brings, all set for life it's said
But what about the things you'll need to help you when you're dead
You've all things that money brings, you can't take when you die
But what about what matters most, the things you cannot buy

Every one will die but very few will really live
In fact some die before they're dead, no dreams to get or give
Others gain the whole world, yet they lose their souls and cry
They're stuck in hell 'cause entrance into heaven we can't buy

Honesty, integrity, too many still deny
Life after life, the reason to comply
Don't cut the tie that character and conscience can supply

Time Stands Still

Some say time flies when you're havin' fun
Content life's whippin' by
But they seldom smell the roses
They're dead before they die
Some think good music's made with notes
Each measure crammed so tight
But it's not breath out but breathing in
The silence makes the hit songs right
It's never what we do but who we do it with the thrill
We need someone to hold us in their arms until we chill

When I'm in your arms I live a lifetime every single day
When I'm in your arms my troubled waters still and calmly stay
When I'm in your arms I care not 'bout the past or future thrill
When I'm swept away in your loving arms
Time stands still

Some say time runs the universe
It measures what we do
It even tells us each our age
The years we've traveled through
But it's not how old, it's how we feel
At six or ninety-five
That measures if we understood
And were fully alive
It's never what we do, but who we do it with the thrill
We need someone to hold us in their arms until we chill
You do much more than hear, you listen in between my lines
You do much more than see, you look for things my soul defines
You stop my spinning wheels and calm my world until I feel
In your arms is the only place on earth where time stands still

Time to Rhyme

Every time my love life's not sublime, fills with slime, grime,
And I ain't got a dime, what a crime,
It's time to rhyme

Cliché used to say, words play a name game, no shame,
Just givin' fame to a dame through rhythm chime
It's time to rhyme

Time to rhyme, no phone or faxin'
Lookin' for some action, Jackson
Please, Louise, yeah jump back Jack
This Dan the man can never slack
Kate don't wait, and Rose knows Chris's kisses I don't like
'Cause Kelly, Donna Karan smelly make me be like Mike

When Sherry, Mary, quite contrary have a man plan they can
Have Dan, like lemon with lime
It's time to rhyme

Tonja, scoping on ya, also Ann ran, then Wayne, so plain
From Brooke refrain, Marie's flee, can't mime
It's time to rhyme

Kelly, belly, Sansom, held at ransom, by yes 'em are some
Peaceful, mellow, yellow, Elyseé style, smile I'm love struck numb
Deb don't fib, Sam can't scam, Paul don't stall, man will need a plan
Time to rhyme, it's KC, for me, wish, dish, Ruby's choice for Dan

True and Trusted Friend

When winds of gossip blowin' singe your mind and chap your heart
When rains of failure beat you down and drench your will to start
When floods of fear near drown you, confidence is sinking fast
Oh, where's the sunshine hope, will stormy weather last?

I am shelter, warmth, that ray of sunshine love can send
I am comfort, courage, loyalty, my strength won't bend
I am deep devotion, you, your honor I'll defend
I am friendship, true and trusted friend

When snows of lies pile up and flakes have covered you in doubt
When blizzards blinding poor perception cloud what life's about
When temperatures drop, bringing on cold shoulders from the past
Oh, where's the sunshine hope, will stormy weather last?

True friend for all changing seasons, true friend as it goes
Always there to take you in and out of weather woes
How to handle elements that no one ever chose
Friends are friends forever when each knows . . .

'Twas Heaven There with You

If I should ever leave you whom I love
To go along the silent way to dust
I am loving you just as I have
And watching you with wanting eyes of lust

Never let the thought of me be sad
Nor speak of me with tears, but laugh and talk
Of me as if I were beside you there
Though out of sight, I'm with you on your walk

I'll be with you when you hear a song I love
I'll be in every rainbow from above
So many things I wanted still to do
To show my never-ending love for you
We cannot see beyond, I know not where with faith I go
But this I know, 'twas heaven here with you, I loved you so

Leaving you, for me, was hard to face
I would stay could I but find a way
Remember that I did not fear, just hurt
To be apart for longer than a day

Grieve me not for this is not good-bye
I only say so long for a little while
The veil between the other side is thin
Until we meet again, there's no denial

What's It All About?

The television news is usually negative and sad
Ninety percent chance for rain
An airline pilot crashed the plane
Gangland violence so insane
The world's a chocolate mess, the outlook, bad

Why not be more positive
Like chance for sunshine ten percent
Ten thousand airplanes safely went
The Boy and Girl Scouts what they've meant
We cannot give up hope in how we live

What's it all about?
The causes of true happiness we learned before age eight
What it's all about we know, so let us celebrate

Laughing, loving, hugging lots for no apparent reason
Singing in the shower, playing dress up every season
Holding hands when we cross streets and taking naps right after treats
Please and thank you, watch the swears, hold some doors, and pull
    out chairs

Choosing good friends, knowing best friends bring out the best in you
Celebrating differences, respecting good things others do
Doing right just 'cause its right, saying prayers with faith each night
There's no doubt, let's change and shout
This is what it's all about, this is what it's all about

When You Love You

I was starving for affection
Yet you walked right by me, looking for yourself
All I needed was a little attention
Yet you put our time together on a shelf

Tell me, don't you know you gotta look inside
Don't you know you gotta open wide
To find you, know you, show you to yourself so you won't hide

Love begins with you
Like a row of tumbling dominoes
The first move holds the clue
Like a dark room with no lights on till you flip the switch and do
Love begins with you, love begins when you love you

I was looking for connection
Yet you stopped just short still searching for yourself
All I wanted was a little reception
Yet you kept your feelings high upon a shelf

Tell me, won't you ever let your heart decide
Won't you ever let your games subside
To feel you, see you, be you till your love can be applied

The natural law of love is that you reap just what you sow
You must possess a gift before you give away, you know
Loving isn't holding back, it's looking in and letting go . . .

Who You Did It With

I'm tired of driving down a two lane highway just to have a one
   night stand
I'm tired of playing cards with a five dollar ante and four bucks in
   my hand
I'm tired of leaning on a three legged chair seeking to balance out
   my world . . .
Then I met you and fell in love—you, the perfect girl

Perfect in the way you give me strength with just your touch
Perfect you don't worry 'bout the world and what they clutch
Travel, concerts, walkin' beaches, makin' love, they're myth
Perfect is not what you do, it's who you do it with

I'm tired of flippin' through a hundred channels thinkin' one has
   better scenes
I'm tired of spending three thousand dollars on suits when others
   come in jeans
I'm tired of speeding up to wait at red lights tryin' to win the rat
   race whirl
Then I met you and slowed it down—you, the perfect girl

Doin' it unto others as you'd have them do to you
Is a deeper soul connection only shared when love is true
What, or when, or where you do means nothing till you choose the
   who
They say nobody's perfect, it's true . . .
'Cause no one knows perfection till they've done it with you

Will I See You Again?

There's a feeling stuck inside me 'bout a leader of life's band
You're the one who showed me how to play, and whispered, "Yes you
    can!"
You taught me life, and living love; your wisdom was my friend
Will I see you again?

There's a memory making motion 'bout a beacon burning bright
You're the one who turned my troubled times from darkness into light
Your guiding ray unveiled the way, you counseled till the end
Will I see you again?

You always cautioned at the door, "Remember who you are"
'Cause I guess you saw in me what I could be
I needed you to need me and you stretched a helping hand
Unselfishly, so tenderly left footprints in my sand
You let me understand

There's a notion nestled in me 'bout the rules of the Master Man
Even though you lost the battle here, you won the war, His plan
I'll miss your hugs and eyes that grin, but we'll meet once more, so
    long till then
When I see you again
Yes, I'm gonna see you again

Winners Make Others More

Was a fifty yard dash, at an Olympic race
Three special people, with courage and grace
Two were in wheelchairs, and one runner stood
At the sound of the gun all three gave all they could

Jenny went weaving, but would finish the race
Joe's chair hit the wall, stranded in place
Kim ran ahead yet with ten yards to go
He looked back to check up on Jenny and Joe

Winners and losers aren't made with a score
It's not who's the fastest, it's deep to the core
It's never just sometime but an all-the-time thing
It's how much we give, and it's how much we bring
Winners and losers aren't made with a score
Winners make others more

Seeing Joe's chair stuck, Kim stopped and turned
The fans went real quiet, as they saw his concern
Kim ran to help Joe, and pushing his chair
Together they finished the race as a pair

Jenny had won it and second was Joe
Because Kim was pushing, he took last you know
Yet the crowd started cheering, and chanting Kim's name
With tears they now knew the real goal of life's game

It's that "something more" that makes us rare
That "something more" that winners share
Aware through "something more" we dare to care

Won't Need More than Each Other

They say we're gonna need a giant ranch to ride the range
They say we're gonna need a million dollars just for change
They say we live to work so we can buy more than another
But I can see that you and me won't need more than each other

With each other we're worth more than money
And our house becomes a home
With each other all our days are sunny
For fun we need not roam
With each other we're complete and whole, and in our love discover
That we won't never need no more, no we won't never need no more
No we won't never need more than each other

They say we're gonna need careers to feel fulfilled each day
They say we'll need a country club for entertainment play
They say we need a lot of things, but all they do is smother
The fact the only thing we need is loving from each other

You Need a Woman, Not a Song

One night I phoned the DJ to request of her a song
A little rhythm for my blues and a melody that turns me on
Stir me with some classical, with a mix of jazzy smooth
I need a little country cryin' slide to mellow out my mood

It needs to rock me every day and roll me all night long
She said, boy, you need a woman, not a song

You need a woman, not a song
Who with a touch can sense what's wrong
Who doesn't love 'cause you're all that, she loves you 'cause she's
    strong
She'll listen in between your lines, and miss you when you're gone
Oh yeah, you need a woman, not a song

I hung the phone up thinkin' 'bout a woman's melody
Composed by God in the key of love, like a beautiful symphony
Could just her single kiss, sustain me all day long
And would makin' love have tempo changes—sometimes slow and
    sometimes strong

I remember, yeah—it's been way too long
. . . I need a woman, not a song

A woman doesn't love you 'cause you're beautiful, you're beautiful
    'cause she loves
Even in the thick of thin things, no one loves you like she does . . .

Party / Fun

Here After I'm Gone

There's a lot of talk about hereafter
Preachers claim it's more than this disaster
More than what, no time like this
Young and restless, often dissed
Many things, won't want to miss

All I want is now, good times and laughter
What about us, what's hereafter . . .

If you're not here after, what I'm here after
You'll be here after I'm gone
With a one chance life, in a lifetime of chance
Waiting seems so wrong
If you're not into action, with natural attraction to finish right now
    strong
Then you're not here after, what I'm here after
And you'll be here after I'm gone

There's a lot of hope for a hereafter
Those who hate their life want it much faster
Hope for love, here after real
Worth the wait, says who, appeal
Where's the party, here's the deal

All I want is now, good times and laughter
What about us, what's here after . . .

After I'm gone, here after, I'll keep my groove on
And you'll be here, with a past that's clear, with chances gone
But never fear, there's always here after here . . .

Party PhD

They say you've got to study, prepare to get a job
That school will give you options, no one hires drop-out slobs
But courses in my major were not offered which seemed strange
So I wrote my own curriculum and recommend this change

High school's overrated though I gained a lot of knowledge
Everything I need to know, I learned those seven years while acing
    college

Always remain seated while the barroom spins around
I read drinking's bad, so I stopped reading, how profound
Twenty-four hours in a day, with twenty-four beers in a case,
    coincidence?
No, but don't you drink and drive or putt, it makes you tense
At the clubs go ugly early, dance the monster mash
The only thing she needs to be the perfect babe is cash
Join a frat and play, most honor students work you know
For the C students who stayed out late, they now call CEO
Marry money, laugh, the school professors envy me
And it's all because I'm a graduate with a party PhD

They say you've got to pass your classes, cheating never pays
So I sucked up to the nerds so answers were just seats away
They say my Bud Light breakfast, lunch at Hooters was real strange
But the wisdom I learned grazing there is nothing I would change

High school's overrated though I gained a lot of knowledge
Everything I need to know, I learned those seven years while acing
    college

Won't Be Coming Back

(Sung by a woman)

One night a couple started out to share a lovely dinner
But quickly turned into a fight that soon would crown a winner
When he confessed his love affair it triggered in his wife
The side that hyperventilates with threats of limb and life

She got that look she caught a crook, arrested him with her eyes
As judge and jury sentenced him with death row bad good-byes

If you run off with my best friend I'll really miss her bad
When you were born the doctor spanked you, should have slapped
    your dad
You said you'd change your worthless ways, your dreams were
    always stalled
Whatever job you did made nothing, work it can't be called
You lazy, cheatin', home wrecking jerk, you infidel, lyin' sack
With your verbal abuse and your hormones loose,
I won't be comin' back!

"May I buy you a drink so I look better?" he begged like a whipped
    little beast
She scoffed, "Beer's the reason we ever made love, you're ugly, a six-
    pack at least!"
"Forgive me, I love you," he whimpered with tears, "She never
    meant nothin to me"
She screamed, "Now you know what I've thought about you,
    please put *you* out of my misery"

Love? Huh? Blessed from above? Exchanged for a bimbo's sighs
Then she yelled that his parents were not ever married, repeating her
    bad good-byes

Trophy Wife

An older married man declared that he and his wife actually shared
Some seventeen good years of blissful marriage
Seventeen out of fifty-five ain't bad, he winced, yeah I've survived
but had affairs since dates in horse and carriage
A forty-year-old man divorced, his mid-life crisis took its course
Not happy he went searching for some more
Bought a sports car, lifted weights
Thought tanning beds would get him dates
But nothing helped 'cause one thing he ignored

Both want it all, want a happy life
Both should have married a trophy wife

I held out for a ninety-year-old billionaire
Who had a bad cough, died in just a week
I cleaned her teeth and washed her hair
Wrote her will to show I care
All before she woke to show her love is what I seek
You can marry more money in an hour than working all your life
There she is cremated in an urn
I'm wealthy with a trophy wife
Up on a shelf, in a polished urn
So proud of my trophy wife

I deserve to live the life of luxury with no strife
'Cause I've worked my fingers to the bone for others
Spent a lifetime planning for a payday as a gold digger, I say
I'll find her assets like a mother's

She'll be old, a cheerleader for Ben Hur
No I won't be a centerfold, she'll only want my company
It's time for me to settle down, retire from the run around
I've got things money can't buy, hear my plea

No disgrace in wanting all in life
You can too with a trophy wife

Heaven for Seven on a Good Old Boys Night Out

At six o'clock a knock on Green Street's door begins the night
Seven mellow men now meet again, a monthly sight
Food and drink still help them think and reminisce the past
And monitor the memories of glory days that last

Born in '55, their history's long, their stories prime
The conversation moves to Monsen's home, it's Miller time
Golfing, houseboat, football games, adventures all, no doubt
But it's heaven for this seven on a good old boys night out

Chilton's playin' Jesse Collins Young and Springfield blues
Morgan's table talking, teaching card games he can't lose
T.J.'s hiding rat-holed chips while Ogaard cooks the books
Clark is jokin', Monsen's blue flames smokin', while we look
Dunn's home brew is potent, conversations always stout
It's heaven for this seven on a good old boys night out!

They say to count your age with friends not years and you'll find joy
Knowing real friends schedule time for a man to be a boy
"R-F," "Challenge," "Match the pot," laughing till they're numb
Using words like "Glarne" and "Idjo," "Go me," "Em-er-some"

Livin in the past for hours, golden goodies on
Doors, the Byrds, Santana, Neil, the Eagles sing along
Solving the world's problems through their bluffs and Twist and Shout
It's heaven for this seven on a good old boys night out

Some swear they're high school sweethearts, never ever far apart
Not gay, but in the way they are connected at the heart
They love to live and live to love, free spirits on the run
Bob, Todd, Todd, Teej, Dan, Rich, Cary, seven souls yet really one . . .

Pick-up Lines

If I could control the alphabet, I'd put U and I together
Excuse me, can I buy you a drink, so I look even better
Do your feet hurt, "why?" 'cause you've been running through my
    mind all night
What's your sign—my psychic said our stars tonight are bright
I love the swing in your backyard, for your moves I am suited
Here's my card, it's good for dinner, breakfast is included

Lines, lines, pick-up lines
But what's a man to do
When I'm guilty in the first degree, of lusting after you
Milk does the body good but dang, how much did you drink
Trust me, I am shy, your mom would love me, don't you think?
No, I've never done this, by the way my Porsche is blue
I swear these aren't just pick-up lines, God made me just for you!

Pardon me, I've lost my number, can I borrow yours
You're a broom, you've swept me off my feet right out the door
Weren't you at my lottery party, yeah, I won, I'm lazy
Your car's gotta be outta gas, 'cause you've been driving me crazy
Was it love at first sight or should I walk by again?
I'm yours, so what two other wishes will you ask to win?

Wide Eyes

(Sung by a girl)

There's a little saying that you all have heard said
That parents have eyes in the back of their head
If you don't believe it then I challenge you
To visit my family and see that it's true
When my boyfriend comes over to help me with school
And my father's asleep so I'm playing the fool
As soon as I snuggle and look for a kiss
A high-flying shoe interrupts—whoa, just missed
So go to another room now all alone
Then my mother yells, "It is for you on the phone."
So outside we go, where the moon is so nice
But the porch light starts blinking, is there any advice?

Yes! When you're in the parlor and your lips are tightly pressed
And Dad sicks Rover on your man, to bite him to confess
Remember to stay out of sight, don't linger at the gate
For love is blind, but the neighbors ain't
But if by chance you get romance and hide from parents' view
Remember where you hide from them
So you can catch your kids there too!
Yes our parents have wide eyes and know what we can't see
But I'll bet when I'm a parent, I'll protect my kids, like they do me!

My dad warned if girls wore clothes so tight we couldn't breathe
The guys would have the same problem and never want to leave
Mom warned if girls wore short skirts, looking like a wide belt band
Guys will want us for the wrong thing shown in our marketing plan
Parents say the sex monster comes out at night, think twice
And that curfew's for our good, so is there any good advice?

First Kiss

(Sung by a girl)

I remember when I got my first kiss
And tryin' to figure out a way to duplicate this

Then it dawned on me that mathematics was the key

So I phoned my favorite boy, explained the plans I had in store
At first it worked, but he's not hangin' round much anymore

He was teaching me arithmetic, he said it was his mission
He kissed me once, he kissed me twice and said, "Now that's
    addition"
And as he added smack by smack in silent satisfaction
I sweetly gave the kisses back and said, "Now that's subtraction"
Then he kissed me, I kissed him without an explanation
Then both together smiled and said, "That's multiplication"
Then my dad appeared upon the scene and made a quick decision
He kicked that kid three blocks away and said, "That's long
    division!"

We've always known what 'rithmetic was for
In music beats per measured score, in baseball who bats poor

Now it's clear to me there's one more purpose we can see
In kissing, it's the time it takes for the boy to hit the floor
Yeah, we tried again but now he's gone for ever more

'Twas the Night Before Christmas

'Twas the night before Christmas
And all through the house
Things were real mellow
Even Irving, the mouse

Our boots were hung up
The incense was lit
In hope that St. Nick
Would soon do his bit

The tree was decked out
It was really a sight
With love beads and flowers
And a flashing strobe light

Wearing my t-shirt
From Woodstock nation
I was just getting into some
Good meditation

And my chick was doing
Some yoga in bed
Munching a fruit cake
While propped on her head

Then . . . Pow . . . in the light
. . . A hullabaloo
It shook the waterbed
And woke up ol' Blue
I stumbled around
And tripped on my beard
It stuck to my toes
And felt really weird

When I got to the window
I was really uptight

'Cause the scene I perceived
Was a mind-blowing sight!
What through my shades
Did I see through the snow?
But eight tiny mooses
And a wild UFO

With a big dude inside
Looking kinky and groovy
I flashed, "Is this Nick
Or some kind of movie"

They came from the cosmos
Like a far-out caboose
And this fat cat kept yelling
At each midget moose
"Right on Dasher! On Dancer!
Rudolph, you be mean!
Get your bod's in high gear now,
And move this machine!"

Then onto the roof
They flew with a shout
The whole cosmic crew
Really freaked me out!
They caused such a hassle
And made such a fuss,
I thought the fuzz would be
Called on us
But before I could say,
"Hold down that loud jive!"
Nick zapped toward the chimney
Leaped in with a dive!

He trucked from the fireplace
His smile all agleam
I thought, "It's unreal, it must be a dream"
Then he nodded and said,
"This isn't a bummer

Like, I've come in peace
To groove my Yule number"

His duds were all fur
Trimmed in leather and such
And he came in stone funky
He was really too much
His backpack was painted
With black light festoon
Full of albums and posters
And a neon balloon

His eyes a light show
His beard did glow bright
A plastic, fantastic, kaleidoscope sight!
He looked like a guru
This beautiful cat
I thought, like wow!
This dude knows where it's at!

"Don't want to sound heavy"
He said with a grin
"My message is simple
So dig it, tune in
I brought you some goodies
But that's not the thing
My real trip is bringing
Good vibes to this scene"

So we rapped till dawn
About peace, love, and truth
Then he said, "Gotta split
Or I'm late to Duluth"
He wiggled his nose and finished his bit
And straight up the smoke hold
This fat cat did split
As he spun from the roof
And into the air

He yelled, "Get your heads straight
You people down there
Merry Christmas to all
And to all a good night!"
And then in a flash
He streaked out of sight
(really out of sight)

Political/Cause

All in a Smile

(Ode to Operation Smile)

Have you ever seen a mother cry
I mean weep because her baby isn't healthy, knows not why
Have you ever heard a mother pray
I mean plead that her new baby will be whole and well one day

A mother's tears could fill a hundred cups from her child's pain
And yet she never loses hope, her faith remains

Who will love a mother, who will help her child
Who will free a spirit who has been exiled
Listen to the still small voice that whispers make a choice to serve a
    child
And the thanks you get is all in a smile

Have you ever seen a young child's eyes
The look when they're ashamed of what you see, and seek disguise
Have you ever heard a young child's heart
That beats so loud from fear you'll help the others, then depart

A young child's need to feel accepted, wanted, whole is real
And so they never lose their hope, that you will feel

Faces from so many places change and smile and glow
A smile will take your heart to places words can never go
Who they were before is just a memory they know
One smile at a time, we can heal the world and so . . .

Walk in Their Shoes

Is an Indian wrong, when the words to his song
Are "my heroes grow up to kill cowboys"
Is a black man to blame for despising the shame
From the blind, blue-eyed devil's mad noise

Does God really choose between Arabs and Jews
And their real estate profit and loss
Must the Irishman fight over which church is right
While they kneel at the same bloody cross

No, no, till you walk in their shoes you can't know, know
It ain't easy, they're barefoot with holes in their souls
No, no though the same God who made them, made me and you
We can't comprehend till our babies die too
When the school bus blows up, what their mothers go through
No, no . . .
I pray *no* one should walk in their shoes

Should a disabled man be held back though he can
Just because he works different than you
Should a Vietnam vet let Fonda forget
Fifty thousand brave soldiers who died for her too

Should a homeless girl die 'cause she don't qualify
When a suit says she's crazy and strange
Can we keep treating history as if it's a mystery
Believing that things will just change

Save the World

Nine Eleven, thousands of our parents died
Violence in the name of God, Holy War, they cried
Pain and sorrow everywhere, oh God must get the blues
Yeah He's there, but I guess He's left it up to me and you

So don't you think it's time to save the world
Time to heal, time to feel
Don't you think it's time to save the world
We've been wrong for way too long
Let's fly one flag unfurled . . .
Oh, don't you think it's time to save the world

Homeless children need more than our prayers today
They're starving down in Africa, and AIDS won't go away
Weapons of destruction, won't someone get a clue
Stop the madness all children need another sunrise too

We're saving whales and birds and fish
A vintage car and china dish
Famous paintings hung up on the wall
We took for granted peace on earth, and got a wake-up call
It's a small world after all . . .

May You Never Fly Alone

May you always have a cloudless sky ahead
May the wind beneath your wings be prayers we've said
May your HUD show coast is clear, with tanks full you are free to
roam
May you always have a tailwind that will hurry you back home
May you always know we love you and support you, carry on
May you know you've got some wingmen on the ground while you
are gone
Flyin' Mach two, hair on fire, nine Gs, crunchin' breath
Fight, win, Libertas Vel Mors, It's Liberty or Death
B-1, Buffs and Hogs on target, air supremacy
Sorties through the SAMS performed with laser surgery
When duty, honor, country call you deep in the danger zone
May God bless and protect you, may you never fly alone
May you always feel the sunshine's warm embrace
May you soar above the rest with an angel's grace
May you know we think about the sacrifice you daily make
May you know we're proud of you for what you do for freedom's sake
May you always know your service matters now and years beyond
May you know we'll guard the fort, your family's safe while you are
gone
Redtails, Rocketeers, 388th, Gunfighters, Warbirds, 3rd
Numbered 8th and 9th and 12th, 23rd, Creech Thunderbirds
Jumper, Mosely, Hornburg, Fogelsong, Peck, Buchanon, Hobbins,
Carleson
Weida, Coutts, Chief Murray, Blake, Weseloh, Crew Chiefs, Redell
take
Their places as true heroes of the sky . . .
Here's to you my friends, your legacy will never die . . .

Send Your Ship Out

Who made government the Robin Hood of lazy men
Stealing from the rich to give to the poor, then to their kin
Who said life owes anyone a living given them
Especially those who never work, yet welfare rich they've been

Some look forward just to Friday, instead of Monday morn
They think they're paid for being there, their jobs they hate and scorn
They never went to school to qualify the job of dreams
So only get the work left over, pay stays poor it seems

You have to send your ship out to expect one to come in
You have to sow some seeds if you expect some harvestin'
It's not a quick hit, sink or swim, but long term, daily travelin'
You have to send your ship out to expect one to come in

Politically correct is for the children, every kind
None should ever starve or suffer pain or have to grind
It's their parents we should punish, no ambition, effort blind
They make us raise their kids while they fall further behind

Handouts destroy hunting skills, dole starts laziness
While some of us are rowing hard, some ride free, careless
Every man should build his boat, take his oar and fix this mess . . .

Pledge to the Red, White, and Those in Blue

It's early morn, the sun is shining, worry not around
Parents, sons, and daughters working, birds outside the only sound
Suddenly, a tragedy, a crash, a fire lit
Everyone was stunned, and ran outside to see who done it

While everyone was running from the burning building there
The firefighters ran right in, right past them, not a care
And officers raced round to help some folks they never knew
Oh yeah, let's honor heroes, please, God, bless all those in blue

Heroes sent from heaven, dedicated to our cause
Saving lives unselfishly, stay strong without applause
Every color, race, and creed serve, families wait return
Giving everything they have, sometimes their lives we learn
Yeah, they're heroes, pray for them, please, God, bless what they do
Let's remember, let us pledge, to the red, the white, and those in blue

Late at night, the moon full bright, and quiet is the sound
Then suddenly the peace is shattered, hope is hardly found around
Screams with tears, cry come we fear, oh who will help us through
The only one, who's never done, the hero dressed in blue

Real life heroes, every day we take their jobs for granted
Till crisis hits, and we wake up, our views no longer slanted
We all love you, we all need you, thanks for all you do
When we stand to pledge or kneel to pray we think of you . . .

Christmas / Spiritual

There's No Room at the Inn

We've all been to a party for a newborn baby boy
No thought who he is, you just bring TV's hottest toy
Wowed by decorations, gifts, forgetting why you're there
Talk is 'bout the shop sales, sipping cocktails without care

But what if this young boy would one day save the human race
Walk on water, heal the sick, let blind men see his face
What if this young boy was King of Kings and Lord of Lords
Wouldn't we stop partying and pay attention more

Yes you say it's Christ's birthday, a time for peace and cheer
Then why on the list of party guests, does his name not appear

Tinsel, packages, and cheers shouldn't make you cry
But Jesus has tears, he was born to die for you and I
So why would we string lights, ring bells, say reindeer fly
To celebrate his birth, why would we make him share
His earth with some red-suited guy
Yes we call it Christmas, and name it after him
But the way we act is nothing different than it was back then
Until we put Christ back in Christmas and welcome him again
It's déjà vu, we're saying too, "there's no room at the inn"

December starts the season, our favorite holiday
And yet again, we hang our stockings, buy on layaway
Some put up their manger scenes to show how Christmas started
But behind it all the Santa stuff leaves Jesus broken hearted

Yes you say it's Christ's birthday, a time for peace and cheer
Then why on the list of party guests, does his name not appear

Didn't herald angels sing, glory to the newborn King,
Never should we turn away the Christ again
Christmas is our chance each year to say "come in, come in . . ."

The Carpenter's Son

Joseph knew his newborn son was special
Joseph knew an angel gave his name
Jesus would go on to be Redeemer
But how did he learn who and why he came

Joseph must have taught his son of Mary
Joseph must have taught his son to pray
At twelve years old alone he taught in temples
'Cause Joseph's words inspired him each day

Christmas celebrates the birth of Jesus
Virgin mother Mary's honored too
But don't forget the carpenter who taught his son his trade
And all the years of mentoring, the things they must have made
Don't forget example is the greatest way to teach
That Jesus taught what he had seen, then practiced what he preached
Christmas celebrates his birth and everything he's done
Yeah God's his father, but he's the carpenter's son

Joseph must have taught his son to listen
Joseph must have taught his son to love
Jesus knew the law and quoted prophets
'Cause Joseph knew it too, taught from above

Joseph's message fit with his son's gospel
That's why he could be his young son's guide
He and Heavenly Father loved their Jesus
They both wept when he was crucified

Same God Who Made Me Made You Too

I heard the screeching cars crash, hurting child and dad
Mangled next to one another, both were bleeding bad
Dad was white, returning from a meeting of the Klan
Child was black, was thrown out of the other mini van

An Arab doctor stopped, two other rescuers were Jews
One got cut and now no one could tell whose blood was whose

Who decided who has royal blood and whose is who
Are there really four Gods—Racist, Muslim, Christian, Jew
Four Gods in the heavens fighting 'bout what's right for you
No way, they all claim the same Almighty Abram knew
It's one world under one God, indivisible and true
The same God who made me made you too

Two best friends were college roommates, when the war broke out
Called to serve their countries, now at war, their leaders shout
On the battlefield one aimed to shoot around the bend
But luckily he stopped, there in his gunsight was his friend

Stepping over fallen soldiers both sides dead from guns
Friend and foe had bled so much, the pool from both was one

We're all made in the image of God
So which race, color got the nod
Yeah we came on different ships, but we're in the same boat now
Let us pause to question, but then answer with a vow

They Already Crucified Him

A father and his kids were Christmas shopping at the mall
Toy store after store, to find a sold out doll
Everything imaginable his children yearned to buy
Hours later at the elevator he would sigh

Overwhelmed to go to every open house at night
Overweight from tasting every party treat in sight
Pressured to get perfect gifts for each one on his list
On the crowded elevator, mad, he shook his fist

Whoever started this whole Christmas thing should think again
We should track 'em down and shoot 'em on a whim
Suddenly, a voice whispered, "Whoa, news is grim
You're too late, they already crucified Him"

A dad with no money was depressed at Christmas time
How he'd pay for gifts without an extra dime
Then he lost his job, could Santa still arrive
Lost face with family, chose death over alive

When he went to end it all, he walked across a park
Passed carolers through the lights and hid in the dark
Feeling life too painful, harder than he'd heard
Yelled his last complaint, then a miracle occurred

What is Christmas, why Christmas, surely not for elves
It's 'bout the birth of our sweet brother, like no other
And what He came to do that we could never do ourselves . . .

Twleve Twenty Five O-Five

Go away, the Inn is full, there is no room tonight
I know it's cold, and your wife's with child, but I can't help your plight
The Inn man shrugged them off and said the stable manger's free
Then wandered to the warmth of his own bed and let them be

Years gone by, the bells were ringing outside Macy's store
Salvation Army's bucket mostly empty by the door
I walked right by, when a homeless guy gave everything he had
He stopped, dropped ninety cents, and smiled "Merry Christmas lad"

I often think about those nights and ponder those deprived
And wonder if things would have changed
If Christ came twelve-twenty-five-o-five
Humbly now I know that passing by the bells ain't right
And if Christ came twelve-twenty-five-o-five, I'd give my bed tonight

A poor child has no presents, yet believes in Santa too
Her mama prays that the doorbell rings, won't someone help her
    through
I could have stopped but didn't live my Christianity
Yet Jesus taught if you've served the least of these you've now served me

I confess, I now believe
I need Him, not just Christmas Eve
He's my Lord, to Him I reach
Christmas just reminds me I should practice what I preach

Christmas State of Mind

The war was on, the fighting fierce, now in its seventh year
But soon they'd ease their anger, 'cause the holiday was near
The generals told their troops to cease their fire Christmas day
And so they did, then realized it was still a day away

Father'd been away on business, gone for two weeks straight
His little family needed him, but working wouldn't wait
He hustled home for Christmas eve, to share gifts Christmas day
Then realized through time travel change, was still a day away

Christmas can come more than once a year
A baby born in Bethlehem, began a message clear
If one day we can honor foes and love so family knows
Every day can be that kind
It's all about a Christmas state of mind

We sing, let there be peace on earth, and give peace a chance
While politicians play their games of power, land, romance
Summits here and meetings there, they fight to make peace stay
Yet every time they're interviewed, they're still a day away

What if there were no more days except the one today
No other chance to take a stance, no other price to pay
Even if it wasn't Christmas, would you serve and give
Would you be more than you've been, with one more day to live

Christmas state of mind is not religion that you find
It's a way of living daily life, that Christ started at Christmastime . . .

Have a Mary Christmas

There's nothing like a mother's special love
Bringing forth the race of God, in His likeness from above
The pain of giving birth, she says, is worth the joy it brings
'Cause what if the sweet son she bears, grows up to be a king

One holy night a newborn saw her face
Mother Mary cuddled Him, He learned from her amazing grace
In her arms, she prayed for Him and promised loyalty
And God placed in the sky the brightest star to honor Mary

Since that night we know a mother's role is heavenly
Have a Merry Christmas means to be like Mother Mary

Mary's Christmas brought a stable, sacred, quiet cheer
Mary's Christmas taught a deep devotion to those near
Have a Mary Christmas
Have a Christmas just like Mary's Christmas every year

There's nothing like a mother's special love
When times get tough, to get us through, mother's who we think of
Even Jesus turned to her for strength in times of need
And when He died, she wept 'cause in her soul she felt Him bleed

Jesus' birth placed mothers up on pedestals to see
Have a Merry Christmas means to be like Mother Mary

Why do stars say "hi" to mom whenever on TV
Why can moms fix broken hearts, with kisses healing scuffed up knees
What should men learn from their moms that Jesus learned from
    Mary
Make each day a Christmas, giving more makes Christmas merry

Please Put Christ Back into Christmas Please

Ever been to a party for a year-old baby boy
No clue who he is, so you bring TV's hottest toy
Wowed by decorations, gifts, ignoring why you're there
Talk is about the store sales, this babe couldn't care

Nobody knew he'd heal the blind, walk on water, calm the sea
Nobody knew he'd save mankind, that what he said was heaven's key
That's why somebody heard him cry, "This party's not for me,
Please put Christ back into Christmas, please."

They say you better not pout, you better not cry
But Jesus has tears, for you He was born to die
So why would you string lights, ring bells, say reindeer fly
To celebrate His birth? Why would you make Him share His earth
With some red-suited guy?
And while you claim it's all for Him and sing of joy with glee
He cries, "This birthday party's not for me,
Please put Christ back into Christmas please."

Years have come and gone, this wee boy was now a man
A celebration of his life, a showing of his fans
He'd loved us, served and taught us about his kind forgiving grace
And once a week we gathered so his good news we'd embrace
Yet nobody stopped his birthday being twisted spiritually
And when he came nobody made him welcome publicly
That's why somebody heard him cry, "This party's not for me,
Please put Christ back into Christmas please."

Faith

A drought hit the farmland, no rain for a hundred days
Adults scampered into church, one by one each prays
Quickly they all stood to leave, led by the preacher fella
Except for one small little girl, holding her umbrella

A car hit a neighbor child, her bones won't heal, the talk
Adults gathered by her bed and prayed that she would walk
Then they cried and hung their heads, as the doc confirmed bad news
Interrupted by a little boy, holding a pair of brand new shoes

Faith
You gotta have faith
In rainbows we all hope for, with proof of things not seen
Faith
Become as a little child, whatever you conceive
All things are possible, if only you'll believe

My friend's battling cancer, chemo took her hair
No hope for a cure they whisper, adults cry despair
Doctors gave her days to live, but that was months ago
She had bought some concert seats, and wouldn't miss the show

Today she died and left us, her pain had gotten bad
Adults wept and mourned her, especially Mom and Dad
So I told them what she told me, just before she passed away
Be strong, have faith, I promise, we'll meet again someday

Love, trust, pray, pure hope undefiled
You can move your mountains with the simple faith of an innocent
child

Faithful to You, Faithful to Me

(Sung by a woman)

Finding Mr. Right may take me longer
But holding out for everything will give me love much stronger
Sure I dream of tall, dark, handsome, rich, smart, muscles tight
A knight in shining armor, sensitive with gentle might

But more than this, and his great kiss, is a man strong spiritually
Yes my Lord, he will be Yours faithfully

Faithful to the grace You've given
Faithful to Your love
Faithful to high heaven's values, sent from You above
Faithful in the way he knows Your truth shall set him free
'Cause only if he's faithful to You . . .
Will I know for sure he's faithful to me

I know I need a man who has it all
Won't settle for a second best, the reason why love falls
Sure I want someone who listens, caters to my needs
A servant of my soul fulfilling fantasies agreed

But more than feel and passion real is obedience to Thee
Yes, my Lord, he will be yours faithfully

I need a man not just for time but all eternity
Mr. Right means right with God, by this shall all know he
Is the man of my dreams, 'cause he's Yours faithfully . . .

Good Enough for Jesus

Some say I'm the funk in dysfunctional
Some claim I'm the lose in "er"
Some swear when you look in the book of words
Under fail is my picture

I know I should be discouraged
Whenever you put me down
But no matter how worthless you make me feel
My biggest fan is renowned

If I'm good enough for Jesus
Then I'm good enough for you
'Cause the same God who made me
Is the One who made you too
We all will sin, and lose and win
The world sees your flaws too
If I'm good enough for Jesus
Then I'm good enough for you

I labor to learn, strive to serve and think to thank each day
I live to love, love to dream, and always pause to pray
So when you call me names or laugh at me I still stay strong
'Cause my biggest fan says I am right, *you're* insecure and wrong

If you're a racist, sexist, bigot, prejudice is banned
Celebrate our differences and lend a helping hand
No one's a mistake, we're each a part of His great plan
You've got to loosen up, give up your grudge, and understand . . .

Only Heaven Knows

A child sits silent, looking round, a wonder in his eyes
Questioning the world about him, full of pure surprise
Why is water blue, the grass so green, the sky so high
What keeps water in the lake and how come birds can fly
Why are people black, white, brown, and why's a rose a rose
Really, only heaven knows

Older, he's a father now, with questions still unclear
What's the purpose of this life, and why are we all here
Who conceived this human race, for what, a worship call
God, well who made God, and why be good or be at all
Which religion is the truth that surely one God chose
Really, only heaven knows

Only heaven knows all answers where and why life flows
Interpretation of a book won't change how it all goes
Preachers fight, religions kill, they speak and violence grows
All in the name of answers, that only heaven knows

Why are there religious wars 'tween Muslim, Christian, Jew
When Abraham taught all his children 'bout the God he knew
They argue over prayer and clothing, women's rights and law
And music, dancing, scriptural doctrine, each claims has no flaw
Does this bring rewards forever, how our judgment goes
Really, only heaven knows

What about hope, charity, forgiveness and love
Is this not pure religion, and for all, and from above
Radical fanaticals don't represent God's laws
It's only 'bout our faith in Him and how we serve because . . .

God Bless America I Love

I was watchin' out my window cross the Hudson waterway
I could see the towers where my daddy works each day
Suddenly the planes hit, crumbled buildings, Mommy cried
Nine Eleven millions saw my dear sweet daddy die

Citizens were killed by residents whose hatred's clear
Being an American means more than living here

Why would someone want to muffle freedom's awesome ring
Nine Eleven just reminds us why we all sing

God bless America the beautiful I love
As long as we are righteous we're protected from above
A special place we all embrace with liberty for all
Always strong, we'll carry on and rise each time we fall
God bless America the beautiful I love
God bless America I love

Hundreds at the Pentagon were blindsided that day
Heroes on Flight 93 took charge, "Let's roll," they say
United we stand stronger against all evil, make them pay
Freedom is a gift from heaven no one takes away

Please oh please don't get me wrong, it's just a twisted few
Claiming Muslim, Christian, Jew, McVeigh, Bin Laden, Judas too
Is this real religion, killing people, get a clue
I wish the bad guys loved their daddies too

Mine eyes have seen the glory of why we're the promised land
Discovered by men led of God, then founded on God's plan
Free agency to choose our destiny is our main thing
No one should mess with us, we'll never lose, we proudly sing

Believe

I remember as a boy, I lost a tooth one day
Put it underneath my pillow, so the Tooth Fairy would pay
Later on that April came an Easter holiday
Where a bunny brought her chocolate eggs with a scavenger hunt to
    play

And then of course December came with claims on Christmas Eve
That Santa would bring gifts to all the good kids who believe

Believe, they say all things are possible if you believe
Money for a molar, hidden treats a rabbit leaves
Presents underneath a tree, things we've all received
And the reason they all happened was because we believed

They say that seeing is believing, oh how wrong they are
Believing keeps us seeing out of sight things near and far
Like gravity, the wind, the sound wave music in our car
And praying to an unseen God or wishing on a star

We can move our mountains, heal the sick and part the sea
Faith precedes the miracle, it's all about belief

Believe in life, believe in love, believe there's help from God above
Believe in dreams, believe in you, believe you'll make it through . . .

Conscience

Talk to God today, my friend, and avoid the Christmas rush
The key to morning, the lock at night
Is a prayer and a moral flush

Sin will keep a man from praying
But prayer keeps man from sin
If you were arrested for being a Christian
Would the evidence convict you again and again

Religion is a personal thing between your God and you
But to help you, guide you, walk beside you
God gave conscience too

Conscience!
Makes you worry 'bout the things it couldn't stop that you have done
Conscience!
Makes you fear that people will know, so do not do it though it's fun
Conscience!
Makes you sense it's wrong and tense to live your life as a moral dunce
There's no pillow quite so soft . . . as a clear conscience

A man with inner noise and demons is not free to live
A lamp can only give light when it has it's light to give
It's what you do when no one is around that makes you good
Doing right just 'cause it's right, just 'cause sweet Jesus would

There's no temptation sent your way that you can't handle fine
'Cause God gave you a constant conscience, you can toe the line

Conscience will not fail you, only you can block it out
If you feel far away from God, it's you whose moved so turn about

Thirty Years

1973 seems like yesterday, so clear
Relieved 'cause I thought seventh grade would be my senior year
Memories of mornings in the front hall right away
To hear who got arrested and the gossip of the day
Homework, formal dances, stomps, and practicing to play

Against the rival Rams and South High Cubs for Leopard pride
Then after games, at Arctic Circle, hard guys would collide
Accapella, drama, sports, ROTC choices wide
Some got real involved while some were shy, their dreams they'd hide
Confidence not talent was the thing that would decide

Sex, drugs, rock 'n' roll was the '70s culture core
That's why my cholesterol count is more than my SAT score
Why some were sophomores twice and Queen of Prom at twenty-four
Why pharmacists at school could sell vacations during war
Why some thought flexible scheduling was for ski buses we'd board

Yeah some of us were late to bloom 'cause we blew classes off
Thinking I'll just marry a ninety-year-old billionaire with a cough
Most, however, studied, climbed to education's loft
With discipline they learned from Lefty Bennett, Mr. Croft
Now living proof that they were solid strong when once thought soft

Whatever group you fit in then, would you change senior year
I'd risk more, love more, judge less, yes and listen, not just hear
I'd pick a better batch of seeds to sow with my same peers
Forgive those who had hurt me 'cause it's how they dealt with fears
And live each day 'cause past is gone, the future's spotless, clear

On our tenth reunion curiosity fed doubt
Wondering who had rented fancy cars to fake us out
At the twentieth we saw old flames and hid our stares
Thinking, whoa, I'm glad I'm not with him, thank God for
    unanswered prayers
Double whoa, his toupee's just a strand of long ear hairs

But now we know it's not our dough, or being babes and steers
It's being real with family, friends, let's raise our glass with cheers
Here's to us, when school burned down, the ones who never veered
We, the next year's senior class, stood strong with laughs and tears
Growing up with you was great as grey hair now appears
So here's to you, my long-time friends, and to our next thirty years!

—August 8, 2003, East High School Reunion